Winning
in the Wilderness

FOREWORD BY JON GORDON

Winning
in the Wilderness

15 Truths for Uncertain Times

Dr. Arlie Whitlow

XULON PRESS

Xulon Press
2301 Lucien Way #415
Maitland, FL 32751
407.339.4217
www.xulonpress.com

arlie@rootschurch.tv / 703-283-0303 (cell)

Unless otherwise indicated, Scripture quotations taken from the Holy Bible, New International Version (NIV). Copyright © 1973, 1978, 1984, 2011 by Biblica, Inc.™. Used by permission. All rights reserved.

Scripture quotations taken from The Message (MSG). Copyright © 1993, 1994, 1995, 1996, 2000, 2001, 2002. Used by permission of NavPress Publishing Group. Used by permission. All rights reserved.

Scripture quotations taken from the English Standard Version (ESV). Copyright © 2001 by Crossway, a publishing ministry of Good News Publishers. Used by permission. All rights reserved.

ISBN-13: 978-1-6628-5087-5

Table of Contents

Foreword

Years ago, a friend gave me a CD, and it changed my life. It was a recording of a sermon by Pastor Erwin McManus called "Why I Follow Jesus." The message moved my heart, and I committed my life to Jesus. A transformation took place in me, especially in my outlook and attitude. I started becoming more of a positive person.

I became a member of Mosaic in California, where Erwin pastors, and later a board member. However, my home is in Ponte Vedra, FL, and I wanted to find a local church to connect with and support.

In June of 2020, our staff came together to do an in-person training event in Jacksonville, our first since the pandemic shutdown. One of our incredibly talented staff, Amy Kelly, invited the team and me to visit a brand new church. She said the new pastor was the son of her long-time pastor in the Washington, DC area.

On that Sunday, the crowd was sparse. I think there were like five people in the room! But Arlie shared the vision of Roots Church with conviction. My heart again was stirred.

After the service, we went out to talk in the parking lot. Arlie came out and introduced himself. He shared how my books and podcast, Positive U, had been a great encouragement over the years. That's when I looked at my watch and noticed the time – 11:11 AM. Those are special numbers for me. At that moment, I knew God was speaking to me, calling me to support Roots Church.

I know the growing Jacksonville area needs another life-giving church. I'm excited to be a part of building something from the ground up. I had no idea Arlie was also an author. After reading the manuscript, I knew this was a message for our day.

The mission of my life is to encourage millions of people one person at a time. That's why I want you to read this book. Every page contains encouragement for your soul. If this message helps you, please share it with someone you know. And, if you're ever in the Ponte Vedra area, stop by Roots Church one Sunday. I'd love to say hello.

Jon Gordon

Special Thanks

I want to say a special thanks to Jon Gordon. After reading his books, *The No Complaining Rule*, and then *The Energy Bus*, I started to write, with the hopes of finishing a book several years ago. Also, his podcast – *Positive U*, has been a great source of inspiration. I had no idea Jon and his wife Katheryn lived in Ponte Vedra and would one day become part of Roots Church. Only God does things like that. In his perfect time, he sends the right relationships our way to encourage us to finish what we began. I also want to thank Amy Kelly, a talented author, consultant, and member of Jon's team, for her invaluable input. With so much going on in her life, she took her precious time to mark up my manuscript. To my brother-in-law, Dave Vanderluct, thanks for your helpful comments as well. You all are full of encouragement! I'm also grateful for the editing skills of Sherrie Irvin. Also, a heart felt thank you to Nisha Marvel. Your corrections and advice took this book to another level. Finally, I want to thank my precious wife of 23 years, Wendy Whitlow. She constantly challenges me to go further than I thought possible. I love you!

Introduction

S itting around the fire pit under the deck, we shared memories of dad while waiting for him to die. After spending the day in the living room around his bed, we needed fresh air. No longer tethered to all kinds of life support machinery, only a single oxygen tube sat softly on his upper lip. Dad couldn't swallow, and his body was shutting down, like power to a warehouse, one breaker at a time.

The yellow flames shot through the metal mesh barrier of the fire pit, forcing us to fold up our outstretched legs. With nothing more to say, we sat and stared at the glowing, orange nuggets of coal in the center. Someone opened the door and encouraged us to make one final visit before he passed.

A couple of days before, we had spoken to the doctor and heard for the first time, "Your dad is dying." We pressed for a solution. How about a feeding tube in his stomach? What about reducing his sedatives? The doctor listened, but said like an old car dad's body was worn out. Every time he fixed one issue, three others would break down. Then he said dad was in another normal season of life. Just like learning to walk, going to school, getting married, having a family and career, dying is an inevitable part of living. Instead of prolonging his pain, he encouraged us to celebrate his life.

The living room, once vibrant with chatter and activity, was now dark and quiet. There lay the withering body of the person who had the greatest influence on my life. I took a knee by the bed and clasped his cold, pale, wrinkled hand. Looking into his half-opened eyelids, the mouth that normally smiled warmly now gapped to one side as he labored to breathe.

The doctor told us to share our hearts because his unconscious mind was still aware and listening. With no idea where to start, I said, "It was an honor to be your son. You were a wonderful father. You took great care of mom. It was a joy to work by your side for seven years. I loved having my office across the hall from yours. Thanks for the memories."

Then the tears came, and I went to a place I didn't expect. "I only wish I could have enjoyed you more. I wanted to prove myself and impress you more than I wanted to be your son. I know you wanted me to chill out and enjoy life but I didn't know how. I missed the opportunity to be closer in our friendship because I took myself too seriously. I'm sorry. Dad, I still want to be like you. I want to love others and live like you did." Just 24 hours later, dad's journey would come to an end. I'm thankful for his example, and for the opportunity to see him off to his eternal home in heaven.

Like my dad, we're all on a trek, walking through the seasons of life. It's worth noting, before the followers of Jesus were called Christians, they were known as "followers of the Way" (Acts 9:1-2). The Bible says we are pilgrims traveling through a land that's not our home (1 Peter 2:11-12). So Second Corinthians 5:7 exhorts us to "walk by faith not by sight." With every decision, we're taking steps. On this side of eternity no one ever arrives. We're all walking toward the Promised Land. Everybody participates.

Like we need a Fodor's Travel Guide before taking off around the world, we need examples to follow. Thankfully, the Bible is filled with them. But one stands out above the rest. Moses spent the last 80 years of his life on his feet, walking through the wilderness. The stuttering shepherd became Israel's greatest leader, lawgiver, and prophet. At the end of his life, the Bible says in Deuteronomy 34:7, "Moses was a hundred and twenty years old when he died, yet his eyes were not weak nor his strength gone."

Winning in the Wilderness is a survival guide. It will equip you to make the most of every season so you can finish strong. This book takes a close look at Moses' life, dividing it into four seasons—Formation, Testing, Leadership, and Sunset. Those four seasons are the four sections in the pages that follow. The chapters in each section have an encouraging truth to help you on your journey. Here are the 15 truths we'll cover.

1. God's good purposes cannot be stopped.
2. Hold on to hope because you just never know.
3. God loves misfits.
4. God can fill our inadequacy with his sufficiency.
5. For every barrier God has a breakthrough.
6. Every time we tell God "no" the colder our hearts will grow.
7. There's a cleansing agent for the deepest stains.
8. Impossible problems are God's opportunities.
9. Trust the Provider more than your provisions.
10. To last you must do less and delegate more.
11. In the wilderness of waiting God is working.
12. God's presence is your lifeline.
13. Believe the good report and you will reach the Promised Land.
14. Make every effort protect God's call on your life.
15. To finish well, start each day with the end in mind.

While digging into Moses' life, you'll also find humorous personal stories and inspiring illustrations from some of America's greatest leaders like George Washington, Abraham Lincoln, Ulysses S. Grant, and Alexander Hamilton.

You may be embarking on an exciting season, or you may be in between, unsure of what comes next. But every season has an expiration date. They come and go. King Solomon put it this way in Ecclesiastes 3:1-3, "There is a time for everything, and a season for every activity under the heavens: a time to be born and a time to die, a time to plant and a time to uproot…a time to tear down and a time to build…"

This book will equip you to travel well. Remember, God is taking you somewhere, somewhere greater than you could ever, possibly imagine (1 Corinthians 2:9). So, let's get started.

No Matter What Comes Your Way
15 Truths for Uncertain Times

Formation Season | Testing Season | Leadership Season | Sunset Season | Promised Land

(Unexpected Change and Transition)

1. God's good purposes cannot be stopped.

2. Hold on to hope because you just never know.

3. God loves misfits.

4. God can fill our inadequacy with his sufficiency.

5. For every barrier God has a breakthrough.

6. Every time we tell God "no" the colder our hearts will grow.

7. There's a cleansing agent for the foulest stains.

8. Impossible problems are God's opportunities.

9. Trust the Provider more than your provisions.

10. To last you must do less and delegate more.

11. In the wilderness of waiting God is working.

12. God's presence is your lifeline.

13. Believe the good report and you will reach the Promised Land.

14. Make every effort to protect God's call on your life.

15. To finish well, start each day with the end in mind.

The Formation Season

1

Unstoppable

"I know that you can do all things; no purpose
of yours can be thwarted." (Job 42:2)

Our planet travels around the sun at a speed of 67,000 mph. To cover 93 million miles in 365 days, we must move at a decent clip. Cosmologists tell us that the universe is expanding, and thanks to the Hubble Telescope they figure the rate to be 44.7 miles per second. Everything God made is in process. Even rock formations change. Magma moves under our feet in the caverns of the earth. As Little Richard sang, there's, "a whole lot of shakin' going on."

We may try to control our surroundings, but we can't stop the train of transition. Instead of looking at the stars, just look in bathroom mirror. Change is staring back at us. Parents see it in their children. In no time, the legs of our little kiddos soon dangle off the ends of their beds.

Transitions always begin with an ending. Something dies. A door closes. An opportunity dries up. A season shifts. Sometimes it's good, like when your child finally sleeps without a pull-up. But the transitions we notice most are disruptive and difficult.

In Exodus 1 we find a time of disruptive change for the people of God. The cloth on the beautifully set table of their lives was jerked out. Their daily routines and beloved rituals were thrown into chaos. Let's take a closer look, because it sets the stage for Moses' birth and teaches us our first lesson.

The title "Exodus" is taken from the Greek translation of the Old Testament, the Septuagint. Exodus means "going out." But in the Hebrew Bible, the title is *shemot*, which means simply "names," taken from Exodus 1:1, "These are the names of the sons of Israel who went to Egypt with Jacob, each with his family..."

Here is a familiar name—Jacob, grandson of the patriarch Abraham. He and his sons went to Egypt, each with his family. Jacob's sons, who would become the twelve tribes of Israel, are listed in Exodus 1:2-5, "Reuben, Simeon, Levi and Judah; Issachar, Zebulun and Benjamin; Dan and Naphtali; Gad and Asher. The descendants of Jacob numbered seventy in all; Joseph was already in Egypt." Jacob's family, numbering seventy, went to Egypt in desperate need of food during a global famine. Joseph, who was sold as a slave by his jealous brothers, was by then the second most powerful leader in Egypt. He forgave his brothers, saved his family from starvation, and blessed them with a new home in bountiful Goshen.

As time passed, Jacob, Joseph and all his brothers died. However, Exodus 1:7 says, "But the Israelites were exceedingly fruitful; they multiplied greatly, increased in numbers and became so numerous that the land was filled with them." Packed in this one verse are five different expressions for increase: exceedingly fruitful, multiplied greatly, increased in numbers, so numerous, until "the land was filled with them."

Goshen burst at the seams with young families, new housing developments, schools, playgrounds, businesses and excitement. Demographically, their birthrate far outpaced the Egyptians. Everything they did exceeded expectations.

The ancient promise given to Abraham was finally fulfilled in Goshen. Many years before, God had promised the patriarch Abraham in Genesis 12:2, "I will make you into a great nation, and I will bless you." They were living in the season of fulfillment, prosperity and abundance.

To find hope in uncertain times, reflect on this truth: because of Jesus Christ we are the favored and blessed children of God. Galatians 3:7 says, "Understand, then, that those who have faith are children of Abraham." It's no longer about nationality, heritage, or religious tradition. By faith in Christ we are sons and daughters of God.

That's a challenge to comprehend. If you're a parent, think of the love you have for your kids, and how you long to care for them. During COVID-19, our youngest two asked to go fishing in our neighborhood pond. By this time, it was the heat of the day, and I was certain most of the fish were taking an afternoon siesta. With just a few pieces of old bread for bait, the kids began to fish. One of the kids grew tired and put their rod down. I picked it up, put a little ball of bread on the hook, and threw it out by a tree. Bam! A huge fish hit and the fight to reel it in began. Right in the middle, as the drag screamed, my son asked, "Dad, can I have the rod? Can I reel it in?" Now, if a neighborhood kid had asked that, my response would have been, "Who are you?" But I simply said yes because this was my child.

We need to see ourselves as God sees us. Galatians 4:7 says, "So you are no longer a slave, but God's child; and since you are his child, God has made you also an heir." We are not slaves, but God's children. But even more, we are heirs in Christ Jesus. Everything that belongs to God our Father will one day be ours. Remember, you have direct access to God and favor as his child.

But even still, we're not spared from the impact of disruptive change. Exodus 1:8 says, "Then a new king, to whom Joseph meant nothing, came to power in Egypt." With the new king came a new season. He felt no obligation to honor the memory of Joseph. He noticed the Israelites doubling, tripling, quadrupling in size. He studied the projections and in Exodus 1:9 he said, "Look, the Israelites have become far too numerous for us. Come, we must deal shrewdly with them..."

We see his plan unfolding in four stages. First, he sowed seeds of fear and conspiracy. "What if we're attacked and they join our enemies and fight against our country?" (Ex. 1:10)

Second, he stole their basic freedoms and made them slaves. Gifted people who ran businesses, created clothes, and crafted art now worked in the mud while whips cracked overhead. Task masters were employed to make their lives miserable. Exodus 1:14b sums it up, "… in all their harsh labor the Egyptians worked them ruthlessly."

Pharaoh hoped to zap their vitality and weaken their numbers. But to our surprise we read in Exodus 1:12, "But the more they were oppressed, the more they multiplied and spread…" Logically, more oppression produces more weakness. But because of God's favor, it yielded greater multiplication. Every time Pharaoh turned up the trouble God poured out the increase.

No one prays for a disruptive life transition. After the first phase of sudden change, comes the second phase—the season of uncertainty. We have lots of questions. What am I going to do next? How will I get out of here? When will it end? Will I survive? Is this the end? What is God doing? Does God even care? This second phase always drags on much longer than we would like. It can be especially difficult when a person in a position of authority is working against us to make our lives miserable. But let's not lose sight of the promise of Romans 8:28, "And we know that for those who love God all things work together for good, for those who are called according to his purpose." If you feel like some other person or event is controlling your life, please remember this.

Truth #1–God's good purposes cannot be stopped.

God uses the schemes of powerful people and circumstances to propel us toward a better future. Israel had no standing army. Their only weapons were pitchforks and shovels. They found themselves in the crosshairs of the most powerful person in the world.

The Egyptians believed Pharaoh was a god, the son of Ra, great god of the sun. But today, everything he built is in ruins. The big movers and shakers are tiny compared to our God. God had a trump card for every hand Pharaoh played. His schemes only created a back-drop to display God's awesome power.

We know Ulysses S. Grant as the general who took the fight to Robert E. Lee, bringing an end to the Civil War. But when the war began, Grant was over 40 and working for his two younger brothers as a sales clerk in his father's store. He landed there after a string of fail-ures. He had to resign from the army because of a rumored drinking problem. With his dream of being a soldier crushed, he turned to different entrepreneurial ventures in farming and real estate, all of which tanked. To add insult to injury, his own father and father-in-law believed Grant would never make it. However, he had unflagging sup-port from his wife Julia, who knew he was destined for great things.

When the war began (1861), there was a tremendous need for trained soldiers who could lead. As a graduate of West Point, and with experience from the Mexican American War, Grant saw an opportunity. He was given a small post as colonel of the 21st Illinois Volunteers, and the rest is history. The reluctant Grant flew into action while other Union generals sat around and contemplated maps and strategy. Grant famously said, "The art of war is simple enough. Find out where your enemy is. Get at him as soon as you can. Strike him as hard as you can, and keep moving on."

With this strategy, Grant started winning and gained the notice of President Lincoln, who was in desperate need of good news. Just as Grant's star began to rise, jealous superiors took aim and attempted to sabotage his career. Again, he was tarred and feathered as an irrespon-sible drunkard who couldn't be trusted. On one occasion, when his accusers brought up the same tired rumor, Lincoln quickly reminded them of Grant's successes. He said he'd like to find out where Grant got his whiskey so he could send a barrel to his other commanders. In 1864 he was finally promoted to Lieutenant General and stood in command of all the Union forces.

In 1869 Grant became our 18th president, and courageously led the charge to pass the 15th Amendment, which gave voting rights to all citizens regardless of race, color, or previous condition of servitude. In a span of eight years, Grant rose from store clerk to the highest place of leadership in the nation. In the same way, God has a special purpose for us that no adversary can foil. Job 42:2 says, "I know that you can do all things; no purpose of yours can be thwarted."

Back in Egypt, Pharaoh was shocked by the resilience of the Hebrews. So he moved to stage three—a secret scheme to murder every newborn boy. He called two Hebrew midwives, named Shiphrah and Puah, and ordered them to kill every male infant at birth. But these God-fearing midwives disobeyed his command. And when he called them to account, they reported that the Hebrew women were so vigorous they gave birth before they could arrive.

Again, we're amazed to read about their multiplication during such persecution. Exodus 1:20 says, "So God was kind to the midwives and the people increased and became even more numerous." In the ancient world, sowing salt, or salting the earth was a practice used by armies to destroy the fertility of the soil in a conquered land. Pharaoh sowed poison, but God turned it into Miracle-Gro.

Boiling with rage, Pharaoh moved to the fourth and final stage. In Exodus 1:22 he commanded every Hebrew newborn baby boy be cast into the Nile. Soldiers marched through Goshen, stripped male infants from their mothers' arms, and threw them to the crocodiles. This was an attempt to murder a generation, an act of genocide.

But even still, God turned Pharaoh's wicked plan on its head. He multiplied them not in numbers, but by giving them a rescuer. Unknowingly, Pharaoh had set the scene for the birth of Israel's deliverer. As we will see, this tragic moment made it possible for a poor Hebrew child to be raised as a prince in the palace, receiving the most excellent education and training the world could offer.

Exodus 1 shows us how God turned Pharaoh's evil plans upside down to produce increase for his people and to accomplish his eternal purposes. Look at Exodus 1:12 again, "But the more they were oppressed, the more they multiplied and the more they spread abroad..." God wants to do more in your life. Whatever stage of life you're in, he's not done with you. You still have more tread on those tires.

The more life presses, the more God blesses us. Think about the good things pressure produces. Pressed olive oil contains antioxidants, omega-3 fatty acids, and promotes heart and brain health. Wine, the Biblical symbol for joy, can only come after crushing the grapes. Coffee and peanut butter are produced after the bean and nut are ground to powder. Diamonds are created where the pressure is greatest.

The squeezing of our lives is necessary because God knows there's more inside. Like a tube of toothpaste that always has a little more, there's still more God wants to get out of us. In those uncomfortable seasons, we pray with more fervency. Our praise has more passion. Our days have more focus. We find more strength for witness and service. We see our calling more clearly and move out in faith. The more the enemy presses, the more God blesses.

Whisper this prayer right now, "Oh God, do a little more in my life today." Are you feeling pressed at work? Maybe your boss is out to make you look bad. He gave your deal to someone else. Or she gave credit to another for work you did. I'm not suggesting you spend your life in a toxic work environment. But you do not need to be afraid. The more they push you down, the more God will provide and promote. You may sit in their seat one day.

Above all, in the season of uncertainty, make God your number one priority. Think about the pressure the Hebrew midwives felt to compromise. This was their chance to escape, find freedom, and start a new life. All they had to do was follow Pharaoh. But they defied his command and stood their ground

Shiphrah and Puah feared the Lord, much more than they feared the king. They had a holy respect, honor, and sense of awe for God. This world wants to pressure us. The pharaoh of our day wants to squeeze us in its mold. Let's make up our mind to serve the Lord.

If you are in a season of transition, take heart. There is no one like your God. His favor is unstoppable. His plans for you cannot be thwarted. If the door you're knocking on is closed, maybe there's a better one waiting for you to open. See yourself today not as a slave, but as a redeemed child of God. No weapon formed against you will prosper. God's good purposes cannot be stopped.

2

You Just Never Know

"Oh, the depth of the riches of the wisdom
and knowledge of God! How unsearchable
his judgments, and his paths beyond
tracing out!" (Romans 11:33)

In Exodus 2, we meet a courageous couple—Amram and Jochebed. They already had two kids, Miriam and Aaron. In this most stressful hour, when all of Goshen was in survival mode, Jochebed became pregnant. With Pharaoh's command to kill all the male infants under two, I'm sure they began praying for a baby girl. But when delivery day came, out popped a boy. Exodus 2:1-2 says, "Now a man of the tribe of Levi married a Levite woman, and she became pregnant and gave birth to a son. When she saw that he was a fine child, she hid him for three months."

The Bible says, "When she saw that he was a fine child…" Every child is a beautiful miracle from God. Just consider what it takes to bring a new life into the world. Most of the 100 million sperm swimming in search for the egg die on the way. Only a single sperm reaches its destination with the stamina to break through the protective layers.

If the stars align just right…Boom! Scientists have actually captured pictures of the explosion of light the moment the sperm penetrates the egg. The fireworks erupt from clusters of exploding zinc released from the egg at the time of conception.

The fertilized egg still must pass down to the uterus and be healthy enough to attach itself to the womb. By this time cells are dividing exponentially. By weeks 4 and 5, the baby is the size of an apple seed, with a developing heart, lungs, kidneys, brain, and nervous system. Though man and woman lie together, God alone sends the spark to ignite the human soul.

Some contend the starting point for life is about location. Inside the womb, it's only a fetus, or something subhuman. Only when the fetus is outside the womb does it become a human life. Still, others say it hinges on health and viability. Thankfully, God's Word cuts through the fog. Psalm 139:13-16 says:

> For you created my inmost being;
> you knit me together in my mother's womb.
>
> I praise you because I am fearfully and wonderfully made;
> your works are wonderful,
> I know that full well.
>
> My frame was not hidden from you
> when I was made in the secret place,
> when I was woven together in the depths of the earth.
>
> Your eyes saw my unformed body;
> all the days ordained for me were written in your book
> before one of them came to be.

God alone is the giver of life. The good news that you're expecting might be clouded by difficulties. It might be an inconvenient time. You have the wrong job. The house is too small. You're living in survival mode. Or, there are some uncertainties about the baby's health. Amram and Jochebed had no idea their inconvenient little baby would become their deliverer. You never know what God has up his sleeve when life begins. Though every child starts as a tiny seed, God has enormous plans for their future.

Truth #2–Hold on to hope, because you just never know.

Exodus 2:2 says, "…When she saw that he was a fine child, she hid him for three months." Mom made a daring decision. She spent all three months of her precious maternity leave hiding her baby.

Stress. Fatigue. Danger. New baby. The word courageous comes to mind. Courageous means "not deterred by danger or pain." Amram and Jochebed stared danger in the face, and risked their lives to protect their child.

Exodus 2:3 says, "But when she could hide him no longer, she got a papyrus basket for him and coated it with tar and pitch. Then she placed the child in it and put it among the reeds along the bank of the Nile."

When Jochebed could hide him no longer she showed some scrappiness. She gathered papyrus reeds from the Nile and wove a basket, waterproofing it with tar and pitch. Tar isn't something you can just go to the store and buy. You have to make it from scratch. We see in her a spirit of innovation, vision, and creativity.

I think of my parents and their dream to take us on a mission trip while we were in high school. I was a sophomore when they informed us we were going to Lima, Peru for two weeks. We had to tell our teachers, and get all our homework lined up. When I told my JV basketball coach I would miss practice for the next two weeks he just stared at me blankly. With the other team members standing around he said sarcastically, "Hey guys, Arlie is going to go preach the gospel to the naked tribal peoples for the next two weeks." But to my surprise, he supported the decision.

We worshipped with Christians half-way around the world in a different culture. In the middle of poverty we saw their joy and passion for Jesus. It was an experience we'll always treasure.

Here's a great question to ask—What would a meaningful family moment look like? As you present the idea to the kids, don't be shocked if they aren't excited. Parents ignore the huffs and puffs to create experiences to bring the family closer. It doesn't have to be a trip overseas. It can be a bike ride around the block.

Motherhood is under attack like never before. Radical feminist Amy Glass once wrote a blog entitled, "I Look Down on Young Women with Husbands and Kids and I'm Not Sorry." She audaciously declared that raising kids is an easy job for women who have no drive. To Mrs. Glass I would say this. It must be nice to sit alone in your housecoat, sip your latte, and type this kind of garbage on your new MacBook Pro while petting your poodle.

Thank God for courageous mothers! While Jochebed made that basket she was doing the most important work of her life. In Proverbs 31 we find a description of the virtuous woman. She's a creator in and outside the home. She loves and sacrifices for her family. She gets up while it is dark to provide food. She's an entrepreneur, buying land and making linen garments to sell. Others come to her for advice and instruction. Proverbs 31:27-31 goes on, "She watches over the affairs of her household and does not eat the bread of idleness. Her children arise and call her blessed…Charm is deceitful, and beauty is vain, but a woman who fears the Lord is to be praised."

Finally, Jochebed set her baby child on the mighty Nile River. As she did, she put him into the hands of God. Pushing the basket into the rippling water she told her daughter, Miriam, to watch from a distance.

Exodus 2:5 says, "Then Pharaoh's daughter went down to the Nile to bathe, and her attendants were walking along the riverbank. She saw the basket among the reeds and sent her female slave to get it." At the very time Jochebed let go of Moses, Pharaoh's daughter came down for a bath. Walking along the edge, she saw the basket and called for it. When she opened it her heart was moved with compassion.

Quick on her feet, Miriam called out, "Shall I go and get a Hebrew nurse for you?" Pharoah's daughter accepted the offer. In Exodus 2:9 Pharaoh's daughter said to Jochebed, "Take this baby and nurse him for me, and I will pay you."

Two amazing miracles in one. Moses was saved, and Jochebed received pay from Pharaoh to nurse her own son in peace. During that time she prayed over his life, sang songs of faith, and told him about the God of Abraham, Isaac, and Jacob. In the formative years, he heard he was not a son of Pharaoh, but a child of God.

At some point in the parenting process, we have to let go. We can't be helicopter parents, following our kids around the block, hiding behind the bushes. Eventually, we have to put them on the school bus. After sending them off, we can bring our worries and burdens to God in prayer. He loves them and is able to care for them much better than we can.

The time passed quickly. Finally, in Exodus 2:10 we read, "When the child grew older, she took him to Pharaoh's daughter and he became her son. She named him Moses, saying, 'I drew him out of the water.'"

The day came for Jochebed to take the son she bore to Pharaoh's palace. She gave him as promised to Pharaoh's daughter who named him Moses, which sounds like the Hebrew word for "draw out." In God's perfect timing, he drew Moses out of the Nile, and out of Goshen. He placed him with perfect precision in the living room of Pharaoh. He became the adopted grandson of the most powerful leader in the world. He received an excellent education by the brightest scholars, mastering law, history, government, music, and mathematics. Right under Pharaoh's nose, God was training his future deliverer. One day he would stand in that very court and say, "Let God's people go!"

Parents, when everything is against hope, let's keep hoping. Life is like a great game of football. You never turn the TV off until the clock runs out. Doug Flutie might throw a Hail Mary. Tyree might make a helmet catch.

Let's not forget how resilient kids are. When our oldest daughter was just a toddler, we put her in our grocery cart. Rushing into the store we didn't notice she had stood up. We hit a bump and out flew our little girl. She did a face plant right on the parking lot. But after some comforting and a popsicle, all was fine. Off she ran to tackle the next challenge. Kids know how to bounce back. Hardships become the blessings that make them stronger.

Amram and Jochebed had no idea their little inconvenient baby would become a hero. Also, in all the stress, Miriam became Israel's first worship leader, and Aaron the first high priest. Don't pull the plug. Don't throw in the towel. In the chaos God is working out his plan.

The birth of Israel's first deliverer ultimately points us to the birth of Jesus our Savior. When the Son of God was born, his earthly parents were also poor, without influence, living under the dominion of the Roman Empire. When he was a helpless babe, another king, King Herod was also jealous and fearful when he heard the Messiah was born. He too made a proclamation to kill every male child two years and under in the vicinity of Bethlehem (Matthew 2:16-18). As Jochebed had the creative vision to make a floating basket, Joseph had a dream from God to flee Bethlehem in the middle of the night just in time to save the child's life. As Moses' life was saved in Egypt, Joseph and Mary took Jesus to live in Egypt until Herod's death. At just the right time God put Moses in the court of Pharaoh. In the same way, when the time was perfect, God sent his own Son to our world

(Galatians 4:4). Moses would save a nation, but Jesus the Messiah gave his life to bring salvation to all who believe.

Maybe you don't feel very courageous today, and all you see are the mistakes you've made as a parent. Be encouraged. We can bring our sins to Jesus and experience a new beginning. 1 John 1:19 says, "If we confess our sins, he is faithful and just and will forgive us our sins and purify us from all unrighteousness." He alone can deliver us from the weight of guilt so we can fully love those entrusted to our care. So keep hope alive. When God blesses you with a child in a season of uncertainty, you just never know what miracles are on the other side.

3

God's Heart for Misfits

"But where sin increased, grace increased
all the more." (Romans 5:20)

Michael Jordan, also known as "Air Jordan," "His Airness," or just "Superman," was a shooting guard and small forward for the Chicago Bulls in the '80s and '90s. While he experienced moderate success at the University of North Carolina, he took off like a rocket in the National Basketball Association. His achievements include six NBA titles, five-time MVP, and ten-time scoring champ, to name a few. Most impressive, he was a team player who enjoyed passing, assists and playing defense.

But in July of 1993, Jordan's father was murdered while sleeping in his Lexus at a rest stop. Crushed by his death, Michael resigned from basketball to focus on his family. After sitting out a season, he surprised everyone by signing up to play minor league baseball for the Chicago White Sox.

He played his first game for the Birmingham Barons, a White Sox affiliate, on April 8, 1994. I had the chance to see Jordan play baseball in Sarasota, Florida while attending a friend's wedding. Tall and lanky, he looked like a giraffe galloping to first base. It was entertaining, but we all knew Jordan was made to wear high-tops, not cleats. After just one year, he returned to pro basketball.

Have you ever felt like a misfit? As children, this feeling of separateness often comes from a unique physical feature; for example being short, having a birth mark, large ears, being awkward at sports, or having a squeaky voice.

As we get older, the reasons we feel like we don't belong are more complex. It might be a sense of shame from a past failure. Maybe it's feeling inadequate in a world full of overachievers. It could be your personality type. You want to be an extrovert, the life of the party. But when you try you quickly get tired and look for the closest library. Sometimes it's family related. Your family tree is complicated and messy, more like a crazy vine. You're in there somewhere but don't want to talk about it. Or, maybe your parents wanted you to live the life they never did. When you didn't meet their expectations you felt the sting of rejection. Family times are awkward. You feel like a square peg in a round hole, a fish out of water, or like a guy wearing Speedos at a church swim party.

Like we all need food, water, and sleep, we must have belonging, acceptance and connectedness. As God said to Adam in the garden, "It is not good for man to be alone" (Gen. 2:18). When transition happens and life shifts, here's a big question we wrestle with, "Where do I belong? Where's my tribe? Who are my people?"

The last time we saw Moses, Jochebed brought him to the palace and gave him up for adoption. He grew up in the living room of Pharaoh. He learned how to be an Egyptian prince. The Scriptures fast forward through his developmental years into manhood. The next time we see him, he's forty and powerful. He's got bling, influence and swagger.

In a sermon by Stephen found in Acts 7:22, we find this description, "Moses was educated in all the wisdom of the Egyptians and was powerful in speech and action." He had a doctorate in all the wisdom

off her husband to the tune of about $1,300 (about $30,000 today). Many historians believe all of it was a grand extortion scheme from the beginning. The great Hamilton was brilliant but blinded by desire. The revelation of his affair slowly destroyed his influence. His star rose like a Roman candle then quickly petered out. In the end, he was shot to death in a humiliating duel with Aaron Burr (1804) at 49 years of age (See Chernow's book, *Alexander Hamilton*).

How sad, a gifted person with incredible potential, coming to such a disgraceful end. Hamilton's kingdom came crashing down like mighty Pharaoh's. Such career ending disasters do not happen over night, but slowly with one no here and there, until our hearts a callused and cold. How many times did Hamilton refuse to follow the warning signs God put in his path? The Lord graciously reveals his will in many different ways, over and over again. May we trust and obey, giving him the highest place of authority in our lives. Proverbs 3:5-6 says, "Trust in the Lord with all your heart and lean not on your own understanding; in all your ways submit to him, and he will make your paths straight."

Notice again God's command to Moses in Exodus 8:1, "Go to Pharaoh and say to him, 'This is what the Lord says: Let my people go, so that they may worship me.'" God wanted his people free from bondage so they could worship him. Worship is more than sitting in a pew and dropping a twenty. Worship happens when we present all of our life as an offering to God. Take note of the The Message version of Romans 12:1, "So here's what I want you to do, God helping you: Take your everyday, ordinary life—your sleeping, eating, going-to-work, and walking-around life—and place it before God as an offering."

As the plagues progressed in intensity, Pharaoh tried to get Moses to compromise. In plague nine, tricky Pharaoh promised to comply if they only left their livestock. He knew if they left the animals, they would return after worship to their life of slavery. This is how Satan works. He knows his doom is sure, but he will claw and scratch to keep us in his grasp. If he can't get everything, he'll stop at nothing to get us to compromise.

Whatever we accommodate, we grow accustomed to. To train a mighty elephant to obey, all the circus master has to do is tie their sturdy legs to a strong post while they are still young. Soon the elephants accept their chains, and once removed, they no longer run. Their natural, adventurous spirits are broken, and they follow their master wherever he leads. Sin doesn't want to be our buddy. It wants to destroy us. Genesis 4:7 says, "...sin is crouching at your door; it desires to have you..."

I like how Moses responded in Exodus 10:26, "Our livestock too must go with us; not a hoof is to be left behind..." Moses would not concede a hoof. In the same way, we're not to give the devil one foothold (Eph. 4:27). We need that same heart. "Devil you're not getting my cell phone. You're not getting my computer or TV. You're not getting my kids, or my marriage. We've come too far, and been through too much to turn back now. You're not getting my sex life. You're sure not getting my attention. No, not a single hoof. God has done too much for us. I'm not letting you tie me up in any area. I've been redeemed and called to a life of joyful worship. I have a new master now and he has great plans for my life." Just as Moses resisted Pharaoh, the Bible gives us this promise in James 4:7, "Submit yourselves, then, to God. Resist the devil, and he will flee from you."

Finally, notice the transformation in Moses. What happened to the reluctant, insecure, tongue-tied leader? The old hermit out in the bush called down miracles and inspired a nation. The mumbling shepherd responded to Pharaoh's trickery with, "Not a hoof will be left behind!"

What's going on? He grew up a misfit in Pharaoh's home. In his prime, he failed and lost everything when he killed a man and became a fugitive. He was alone in the desert for 40 years, probably convinced his life was over. All of his natural God-given gifts rusted from lack of use. Even after obeying God's call he got into it with his wife. His first attempt to free the Hebrews was a disaster. Let's be honest – he was no Superman. But if God transformed Moses, he can turn any life around. Ephesians 1:18-19 says, "I pray that the eyes of your heart may be enlightened in order that you may know the hope to which he has called you, the riches of his glorious inheritance in his holy people, and his incomparably great power for us who believe."

What is God asking you to do today? Don't be like Pharaoh and refuse to listen. You cannot fight against God and win. Remember, he has great plans for you, to be transformed into the image of Jesus Christ. He wants to free you to live a life of joyful worship. Surrender your heart fully to him, and say, "Yes, Lord."

7

Why the Blood?

> "This cup is the new covenant in my
> blood; do this, whenever you drink it, in
> remembrance of me.'" (1 Corinthians 11:25)

Have you ever asked yourself, "Why the blood?" We see the blood in God's Word from beginning to end. Even Jesus' words are written in red. We can't remove the blood like Thomas Jefferson did when he cut the miracles of Jesus out with a pair of scissors. Instead of hiding the blood, the Bible calls us to celebrate and sing about it. For example, 1 Peter 1:18-19 says, "For you know that it was not with perishable things such as silver or gold that you were redeemed from the empty way of life handed down to you from your ancestors, but with the precious blood of Christ, a lamb without blemish or defect."

I know as a preacher's kid I didn't have an appreciation for the blood of Jesus. In my mind, communion was a snack. Before service, the ushers filled plastic cups with grape juice. In the other trays were tiny, unleavened squares of bread, hard enough to kill a squirrel with a sling shot. At the time, we had a smaller congregation, so there were always leftovers. As the congregants chatted after church in the parking lot, we helped ourselves.

We never served wine, which was good because I would have been plastered. After sitting through Sunday school, we were starving. We gorged on the Lord's Table, stuffing our cheeks with as many wafers as humanly possible. We figured we were doing the church a favor by cleaning up the mess, clueless about the immeasurable value of Jesus' sacrifice.

Some of the greatest songs of faith have been about the blood of Jesus: "Are You Washed in the Blood?" "There is a Fountain Filled with Blood," "There is Power in the Blood," and "The Blood Will Never Lose Its Power." References to the blood can still be found in our popular worship songs. The chorus to the song by Elevation Worship, "O Come to the Altar," proclaims, "O come to the altar, the Father's arms are open wide. Forgiveness was bought with the precious blood of Jesus Christ."

To answer this important question we're going to look at the original Passover. First, let's review. The Israelites came to live in Egypt during a global famine. Joseph was second in command, and helped them get established in Goshen. They started to multiply and prosper. After many years, a new pharaoh arose who hated the Israelites. In one decree he made them slaves. But still they multiplied exponentially. So he made a decree that every newborn baby boy be thrown into the Nile River.

Years of hard labor passed until God raised up Moses. He told Pharaoh to let God's people go, but Pharaoh refused and hardened his heart. So God sent the plagues. Moses visited Pharaoh after each plague with the same command, "Let my people go." But each time his heart grew harder until it was like granite.

Then, after the ninth plague, Moses warned Pharaoh of one last calamity. At midnight every firstborn in Egypt would die. The murderous act against the firstborn of Israel was about to come back on his own head. Still the proud king would not budge.

The final plague was different from the other nine. Up to this point Goshen had been spared, flourishing like a flower while Pharaoh's kingdom crumbled. But the plague of death would come to Goshen as well.

Like Pharaoh, the Israelites had turned away from God. They had forgotten the stories of faith passed down from Abraham, and were slow to believe God's Word spoken through Moses. Also, they gave their hearts over to the gods of Egypt and were worshipping created things and man made objects.

Before going any further, we have to understand a few things. First, God is perfect in holiness. God is loving, faithful, patient, compassionate, merciful, and kind. But, he's also completely righteous, absolutely just, and flawless in perfection. When I think of holiness, I think of sitting on the beach just before sunrise. The tide has washed away all the footprints, holes, and debris like a wet sponge on a dirty chalkboard. It feels like a holy ground, a sacred place as the sun rises over the horizon.

We would never dump our trash, used soup cans, dirty diapers, and rotten food on the beach. The sand, surf, and wildlife are set apart. That's just a hint of the holiness of God. Exodus 15:11 says, "Who among the gods is like you, LORD? Who is like you – majestic in holiness, awesome in glory, working wonders?"

Second, sin is deadly. My daughter has a little plaque in her room. It says, "I'm kind of a big deal." Well, sin is a huge deal. Romans 6:23 says, "For the wages of sin is death…" Notice the picture of a financial transaction. If you work at sin, the wage you earn is death. Eventually sin squanders and destroys our relationships, peace, potential, talents, and abilities. It promises everything up front—joy, release, and self-actualization. But sin always lies.

When I was in eighth grade, my best friend was Jimmy Rosa. Jimmy and I had much in common, like sports and chasing girls. But there was one area where we differed greatly. He was always on the honor roll. My dad, a pastor and lover of history and reading, was greatly vexed at my lackluster grades, and expressed this at each grading period with a stern lecture. After the sermon, my punishment was torture by grounding, usually for one to two weeks. After the pain was over, I was back to my old ways. It wasn't that I didn't understand the material, I just hated homework and never really tried. Every report card day, I felt like I was dragging a skunk into our house by the tail. An idea suddenly came to me walking home from school while holding another stinky report card. I said, "Jimmy, give your mom your report card, and then when she's done let's erase your name and type in mine." This was before the Internet when they sent home carbon copied grades using a typewriter.

To our surprise, the eraser trick worked. In his mom's office, with his named erased, we typed my name in. Triumphantly, I entered our house. My dad was shocked, "Wow! What an improvement. What did you do?" I replied, "Just focused I guess, dad." "Great job, son!"

We couldn't believe it. Our scheme worked. I was free. But after we walked out and slapped high fives, we both were hit with reality. We had to continue lying on every report card day for the entire year. Along with overwhelmed with fear, I had the guilt of knowing I had deceived my father who loved me.

Sin always leads to death. It destroys families and friendships. But even worse, it leads to spiritual death. It separates us from the life of God. It makes our hearts cold and unresponsive. Like the children of Israel were "deader than a doornail" in Egypt, all of us were once dead in bondage to sin.

Psalm 51:5 says, "Behold, I was brought forth in iniquity, And in sin my mother conceived me." Wendy and I are blessed with six beautiful kids. As babies, they looked like perfect angels, but we quickly found out otherwise, especially when they hit the "terrible two's." Instead of a spark of divinity, the Bible tells us the venom of sin is in our nature from the moment of our birth.

Third, we must understand salvation is costly. Because God is perfect in holiness, he can't look the other way, or sweep it under the rug. Like we would never look the other way if someone dumped dirty diapers on the beach. Again, the payment for sin is death. The price had to be paid. Hebrews 9:22 says, "...and without the shedding of blood there is no forgiveness."

Here's the amazing news. When the Hebrews could not save themselves, God provided a way. In Exodus 12, God gave Moses the instructions for the first Passover. Of primary importance was the selection of a lamb. Each family was to choose one. No sick, tired, or lame lambs. Only the best of the best for this special occasion. Then at twilight, the lambs were slaughtered, and the blood was painted on the door frames of the house, on both sides and then over the top. A substitute could stand in their place, dying so they could live.

Here's why we'll never stop singing about the blood. Jesus is our Passover Lamb. In the Bible, Jesus has many titles: Wonderful Counselor, Prince of Peace, Rose of Sharon, Lily of the Valley, Bright Morning Star. Another title is Lamb of God. When John the Baptist saw him coming to be baptized he said this in John 1:29, "Look, the Lamb of God, who takes away the sin of the world!" In a vision of heaven, the apostle John heard the saints in heaven singing, "Worthy is the Lamb, who was slain, to receive power and wealth and wisdom and strength and honor and glory and praise!" (Revelation 5:12)

While dying on the cross, the Lion of Judah could have called a legion of angels to his rescue. But the Lion humbled himself, and became the lamb, dying in our place. The just penalty of death we deserved was placed upon Jesus on the cross. He sacrificed his life so that we could live.

This might shock you, but some blood is more valuable than others. We buy worms at our local gas station for bait. We hook the worm in hopes of catching a largemouth bass. We filet our catch over the garage sink and fry it in a pan—a little canola oil, salt, pepper, flour, and lemon juice. Some of my kids can't believe I would do something so cruel in our home. I remind them how much they love Chick-fil-A.

But think about the blood a mother sheds to bring a new baby into the world. Or the blood, sweat, and tears a father gives to provide for his family. Think about the blood a solider sacrifices to protect our country. But most precious of all is the blood of Jesus, the Lamb of God. Again, 1 Peter 1:18-19 says, "For you know that it was not with perishable things such as silver or gold that you were redeemed from the empty way of life handed down to you from your ancestors, but with the precious blood of Christ, a lamb without blemish or defect."

It took some believing to obey the word of God that first Passover. It was an act of faith, to go public and apply the lamb's blood to the door of their homes for all to see. While they waited, sheltered behind blood-stained doors, the plague of death came. Exodus 12:30 says, "Pharaoh and all his officials and all the Egyptians got up during the night, and there was loud wailing in Egypt, for there was not a house without someone dead."

Finally, stubborn Pharaoh crumbled. He set the Hebrews free. After 430 years, moving day had come. The prison doors were open. Free at last. Time to step into a new beginning.

Notice what God said in Exodus 12:2, "This month is to be for you the first month, the first month of your year." Their whole calendar would orient itself around this salvation experience. In the same way, anyone who has faith in Jesus can experience a fresh start.

Truth #7–There is a cleansing agent strong enough for the deepest stains.

Our family lived for fourteen years in a house with mustard yellow paint. When we moved in we had two baby girls. We quickly grew to six. We didn't really like mustard yellow. It looked like Chick-fil-A sauce all over the walls. But we just didn't have the energy at the time.

Sitting there one Sunday afternoon, watching a bad football game, we just got sick and tired of being sick and tired.

We purchased a nice, neutral color—Agreeable Grey. The new paint contained the heavy duty stain blocker known as Kilz. As we got started, that's when we noticed all the smudges, dirt, grime, boogers, and Lord knows what else. How satisfying it was to apply a fresh, new coat of paint, forever covering the wear and tear from years of abuse.

Those nasty walls are a good picture of the condition of our hearts. Over the years the marks of our sins mar the interior of our lives. But there is a stain remover strong enough to cover the foulest blot. Hebrews 9:14 says, "How much more, then, will the blood of Christ, who through the eternal Spirit offered himself unblemished to God, cleanse our consciences from acts that lead to death, so that we may serve the living God!"

Think about it. The blood of one lamb applied to the door of a home was enough to protect from the destroyer. When death saw the blood, it had to pass over.

If the blood of a lamb could do that, how much more the precious blood of Jesus. The sacrifices in the Old Testament had to be offered continually. People were always messing up. But the sacrifice Jesus made was once and for all. Hebrews 10:12; 14 says, "But when Christ had offered for all time a single sacrifice for sins, he sat down at the right hand of God...For by a single offering he has perfected for all time those who are being sanctified."

The blood of Jesus is so powerful it forever perfects us in the eyes of God. We live in Florida and enjoy getting out to the beach. We've learned to reapply our sunblock every couple hours. It wears off with the water and sweat, and you can end up getting burned. But the blood of Jesus never wears out. We stand righteous before God, as Hebrews 10:14 says, "for all time." While I have issues to work through, and fall short on a daily basis, before God I am perfected by faith in Christ.

That means we don't need to say "I plead the blood" as if it were a magical phrase. There's no need to hunt for a secret formula to chant. When the Bible talks about the blood of Jesus it's a simple but vivid way of describing the sacrifice he made on the cross. By faith, all the blessings of Christ are applied once and for all.

Back to wanting my good friend's report card. I had to lie and pretend his grades were mine. But by faith, the perfect report card of Jesus is ours. Every mark against us is washed in the blood.

Remember, your address has changed. You used to live on Goshen Street in Egypt, the house of bondage. By faith, you moved to Freedom Lane in the Promised Land. There's nothing the devil can do. His power is broken over your life. The blood of Jesus will never lose its power. You forever belong to the Lord. Ephesians 1:7 says, "In him we have redemption through his blood, the forgiveness of sins, in accordance with the riches of God's grace."

8

God Will Make a Way

See, I am doing a new thing! Now it springs up; do you
not perceive it? I am making a way in the wilderness
and streams in the wasteland. (Isaiah 43:19)

There was a time when General George Washington was trapped
and in desperate need of a miracle. In the summer of 1776,
Washington moved his ragtag, volunteer militia of 10,000 to fortify
New York. He knew the British were coming to take the leading city
and its valuable port. The undersupplied, untrained colonial forces,
comprised of kids as young as 15 and grandpas as old as 60, armed
with their muskets, pistols, and rusty sabers, began building forts and
digging trenches.

But their hopes were crushed when 400 British ships set anchor
in the harbor. In total, they had 30,000 experienced soldiers, armed
with the latest weaponry, and over 1,200 canons. After looking at all
the masts in the harbor, one soldier said it looked like a forest of trees
had sprung up in the ocean overnight. The British and Hessian forces
began their advance, and soon Washington found himself trapped at
Brooklyn Heights, with the East River on one side and the Redcoats
on the other.

On August 28, Washington made a daring decision to move the entire army across the river in the middle of the night. It was slow moving all the canons, horses, ammunition, and wounded soldiers. To keep as quiet as possible, they wrapped their paddles in blankets.

As the sun began to rise, there were still troops waiting to cross. In plain sight, the British would move in for the kill. But a thick fog fell across the entire area and hung like a great curtain late into the morning. Every single soldier escaped just before the fog disappeared. When the sun broke through, the British were shocked. Their moment of victory had vanished. The Continental Army lived to fight another day, all because of a mysterious fog fell at just the right time.

Where do you feel trapped today? Maybe you feel the enemy has surrounded you on every side. In this chapter we're going to look at an amazing escape, the greatest salvation event in the Old Testament.

Truth #8—Impossible problems are God's opportunities.

Stubborn Pharaoh finally liberated the Israelites after the tenth plague. Exodus 13:17-18a says, "When Pharaoh let the people go, God did not lead them on the road through the Philistine country, though that was shorter. For God said, 'If they face war, they might change their minds and return to Egypt.' So God led the people around by the desert road toward the Red Sea…"

When moving day finally came, God took them the long way. The quickest route to Canaan was through Philistine country. But their faith was too frail to face the mighty Philistines. If you looked up this route on Google Earth, you would see the quickest way to Canaan was northeast. But instead of going north on Highway 95, God sent them south on a desert road toward the sea.

Exodus 13:21 says, "By day the Lord went ahead of them in a pillar of cloud to guide them on their way and by night in a pillar of fire to give them light, so that they could travel by day or night." Should they ever doubt their direction, the Lord was leading the way in a cloud by day and a pillar of fire by night.

In your life journey, have you ever asked, "Why this way, God? It looks like we're going the wrong way. I thought we were headed to the Promised Land. Why are we on the desert road?"

When everything is uncertain we must have clarity about who we're following. We're not following culture, celebrities, or popular opinion. Like the Israelites had a pillar of fire, we have the Holy Spirit and the light of God's Word. When life doesn't turn out like we planned, and everything is uncertain, let's remember Second Corinthians 5:7 – "For we walk by faith, not by sight." We must trust God's leading even when we don't understand.

The Israelites had a big problem. Pharaoh was spying on them. He was looking for the right moment to send his troops out and bring them back to Egypt. As they wandered south they looked confused, like a pack of lost puppies in a dark alley.

The Egyptians couldn't believe the Israelites set up camp by the Red Sea. Warfare 101 says never camp your army by an impassible body of water. It's like putting yourself in checkmate. But that's where God led them. God said to Moses in Exodus 14:2, "Tell the Israelites to turn back and encamp near Pi Hahiroth, between Migdol and the sea. They are to encamp by the sea." In the Hebrew, Migdol means tower, elevated stage, or raised bed. It could have been a large cliff, watchtower, or walled city.

Pharaoh's spies came back and gave their report, "Why did we let them go? Let's get 'em!" Pharaoh called up 600 of his best chariots. The chariot was a new weapon, a moving platform, able to weave in and out of the battle. While one soldier drove, another could shoot a continuous stream of deadly arrows. It was a killing machine. The newly released slaves had the sea on one side, Migdol on the other, and Pharaoh's army closing fast.

I'm writing this chapter in the middle of the COVID-19 pandemic, and it's created a host of problems. What do we do with the kids when schools aren't opening? What will happen to my job? What about our plans for the future? Should I risk taking my family to church? How do I visit my elderly parents who are at greatest risk? What will happen to the economy? What about concerts, sporting events, and other public gatherings? Many feel afraid, alone, and isolated at home.

You might feel trapped by an old addiction trying to come back into your life. Maybe something is threatening your marriage. You called your momma and asked if you could sleep on her couch. But she said, "No." She told you to leave and cleave. You have nowhere to run. I don't know if it's a fear of failure or a lack of resources, connections, or direction. You just don't know where to go or how to pray.

God spoke to Moses and gave him insight on what he was planning. In Exodus 14:4 God said, "...But I will gain glory for myself through Pharaoh and all his army, and the Egyptians will know that I am the Lord..."

If you're in a fix today, could it be that God has led you to this place? You have nowhere to run. You must be where you are. Maybe, more than comfort, God wants to give you a testimony of his deliverance, power, and grace to share with your children and your children's children.

Pharaoh had gotten all the glory in the past. He was a glory hound. But at the Red Sea God would forever gain the glory. His name became famous as the God who saves his people, the One who parted the sea. If you feel trapped, lift up your head. God is about to give you a reason to glorify, honor, and thank him forever.

Like the bad guy popping out at the end of a horror movie for one last hack, Pharaoh appeared at the Red Sea. The Hebrews were terrified and cried out to the Lord. But they quickly gave up praying and turned to attack Moses.

"Nice one Moses! Why did we ever listen to you! We told you to leave us alone in Egypt. Now we're going to die in the desert!" This was a recurring problem for the Israelites. Whenever a crisis appeared, they quickly threw their faith in the toilet and gave way to complaining and grumbling.

Notice Moses' powerful challenge in Exodus 4:13-14, "Moses answered the people, 'Do not be afraid. Stand firm and you will see the deliverance the Lord will bring you today. The Egyptians you see today you will never see again. The Lord will fight for you; you need only to be still.'"

The command, "Do not be afraid" is in the Bible over eighty times. Clearly God doesn't want his people shackled by fear. Like a virus, fear quickly moves in and takes over. But in the face of fear we can choose faith.

Moses said, "Do not be afraid. Stand firm." In other words, "Don't run away. Don't buckle, beg, and surrender to the enemy. After you've done everything you can to stand, keep standing."

Wherever you feel trapped today, that's God's word for you. Don't run from your marriage, family, calling, ministry, dream, or the impossible situation that has you surrounded! Do what you're called to do even when no one pats you on the back, follows you on social media, or sings your praises. Stand your ground because the Lord is fighting for you, and he is the Mighty Warrior. The battle you're facing is the Lord's, and there is no one like our God! Let the enemy throw everything he has. No weapon formed against you will prosper (Isaiah 54:17). Nothing in all creation can separate you from God's love.

Read again Exodus 14:14, "The Lord will fight for you; you need only to be still." Moses gives two job descriptions, God's and yours. God's job is to fight the battle. Your job is to not worry about his job. You only need to be still. The Hebrew word for "be still" is *charash*, and it literally means to keep your mouth still, cut out the talking, zip it, shut it, nip it in the bud. Notice The Message version of Exodus 14:14,

"God will fight the battle for you. And you? You keep your mouths shut!" Stop freaking out. Cut out the ranting over the worst-case scenarios. Quiet your soul and be still.

I think about the beautiful bird that flew into our garage one day when the door was wide open. It had wings to soar to the heavens, but in that tragic moment, it felt trapped. The bird pounded its beak and head on the windows of our garage. It flittered and fluttered, flailing at the glass. Just before the poor thing broke its neck, we got a broom and gently forced it out the garage door that was wide open the whole time. So often we're like that flustered, little bird, when God is trying to show us a wide door of opportunity. God says, "Stop it. Be still and I will fight for you."

Try it this week. When you feel trapped, surrounded, and left out to dry, get up and go for a gratitude walk. Begin thanking God for all he's done for you. As you start thinking and thanking him, he'll bring fresh ideas to your mind. Psalm 46:10 says, "Be still and know that I am God. I will be exalted among the nations. I will be exalted in all the earth."

Maybe you've wondered, "With Pharaoh's chariot army surrounding them, how did they get away?" Notice Exodus 14:19-20, "Then the angel of God, who had been traveling in front of Israel's army, withdrew and went behind them...so neither went near the other all night long."

Notice the pillar of fire, leading the way out front is now called the "angel of God." The "angel of God" appears several times throughout the Old Testament, to Abraham in Genesis 19:1, Jacob in Genesis 31:11, and Gideon in Judges 13:3. It was the angel of God who spoke with Moses from the burning bush in Exodus 3:2. In each example the angel speaks in the first person for God, and yet it appears to be separate, as God's servant or messenger. Many believe the "angel of God" is Jesus, a pre-Bethlehem appearance of the second person of the

Trinity. The angel stood between the armies of Egypt and the Israelites so neither went near the other all night.

Many have attempted to explain the parting of the waters as a work of nature alone. For example, Hebrew scholar Umberto Cassuto mentions a common occurrence in the Suez region at high tide. The water comes oozing out from under the sand, turning the surface to mud. In little time, the ground is covered in a deep layer of water. The reverse happens at low tide. As the waters retreat, the heat from the sun hardens the sand again.

Emperor Napoleon Bonaparte almost lost his army because of the fast rising tide around parts of the Red Sea. During his tour through Egypt, they crossed over to the far shore without any difficulty. But on their return in the dark, they attempted to cross back but got stuck in the watery sand. In little time their horses were in mud up to their bellies and the tide was rising fast. It was a terrible situation, and many horses were lost. After a great struggle a ford was found that allowed everyone to cross safely.

Many are attracted to these naturalistic explanations. In a similar way, it's our tendency to explain away the miracles of God as time passes and our gratitude fades. The reason we quit smoking is because we just decided to. We experienced a career breakthrough because we worked hard and happened to meet the right person at the coffee shop. The broken marriage was saved because we finally found the perfect counselor. Your life was healed from disease because you pulled yourself up by your bootstraps and became a vegetarian. Let's not short-change God. Your life was saved because he worked a miracle for you!

What happened at the Red Sea for the Israelites was no coincidence of nature. As Moses raised his hands, a mighty east wind fell upon the sea, separating the waters and pushing them up like concrete walls. Exodus 14:22 says, "The Israelites went through the sea on dry ground, with a wall of water on their right and on their left."

There was no way to make a bridge, boat, or a raft. All Moses could do was raise his hands. When we have no one else to turn to, no one to text, or Facetime, we can raise our hands and our hearts in prayer. Our prayers can part seas and move mountains. When we pray in Jesus' name our prayers move heaven and earth. We are making a request based on his authority and righteousness, the name above all names. Jesus said in Mark 11:22-24, "Have faith in God...Truly I tell you, if anyone says to this mountain, 'Go, throw yourself into the sea,' and does not doubt in their heart but believes that what they say will happen, it will be done for them. Therefore I tell you, whatever you ask for in prayer, believe that you have received it, and it will be yours."

Pharaoh fell headlong for the trap, and led his chariots into the heart of the sea. Imagine the panic of the Israelites as they turned back and saw Pharaoh storming after them. But Exodus 14:24 says, "During the last watch of the night the Lord looked down from the pillar of fire and cloud at the Egyptian army and threw it into confusion."

Notice their deliverance came, "during the last watch of the night." Soldiers guarding the camp divided up the night into watches. The last watch was just before the dawn of a new day. Their crisis by the sea lasted all night. Have you ever had a long, dark night in your soul?

During the last watch, God threw Pharaoh's army into confusion. Their horses got stuck in the mud. Wheels started falling off. They began to panic. Before they could turn around Moses raised his hands again and the waters came crashing down. Wicked Pharaoh was buried in the sea.

Let's hold on today. Remember, impossible problems are opportunities for God to be glorified. Many of you are in the last watch. It might seem like the longest night of your life, but a new day is about to dawn. God is going to fulfill his promise.

Ultimately, the parting of the sea helps us appreciate the even greater miracle of our salvation in Jesus Christ. We also were once trapped. On one side was our enemy, the devil, and on the other the record of our sins, separating us from a relationship with God. But on the cross, Jesus made a way through the sea. His death and resurrection became the great bridge. By faith, we can cross the divide and enjoy peace and friendship with God. Our past can be buried in the heart of the sea and the enemy's power destroyed over our life. Have you crossed over yet? He is the way, the truth, and the life (John 14:6).

SEASON 3

The Leadership Season

of the Egyptians, and was "powerful in speech and action." He was the complete package. He had chiseled arms and flat abs. He was comfortable at the table with world leaders. He was on his way to the top.

But like many talented, successful people, underneath the royal robes, he was a mystery to himself. He wrestled with colossal identity questions like, "Who am I and where do I belong? Am I a prince or a slave? Where's my home?" He knew his people, the Hebrews, worked like dogs in the sun, while he sat, eating peeled grapes, in the lap of luxury. The palace parties were over the top—all the wine and women at his beck and call. It was a head rush to be in the inner circle of power. But when the lights went down, and he was alone, he didn't fit in. Surrounded by everything, something huge was missing.

Every person has a desire for self-discovery. That's why we pay big money for services like Ancestry.com®. Their slogan is, "Build your family tree and see your story come to life." One day, curiosity overcame the pressure to conform, and Moses went for a walk to see his people.

Exodus 2:11 says, "One day, after Moses had grown up, he went out to where his own people were and watched them at their hard labor. He saw an Egyptian beating a Hebrew, one of his own people." He stood and watched as his people struggled. Then, he saw an Egyptian beating a Hebrew. A flood of anger shattered a hidden psychological barrier. Exodus 2:12 says, "Looking this way and that and seeing no one, he killed the Egyptian and hid him in the sand." Maybe he clobbered him over the head with a wooden beam or snapped his neck with ninja-like precision. But after taking care of business, he buried him in the sand.

What was he thinking? As a prince, a simple command would have been sufficient. Acts 7:25 gives the answer: "Moses thought that his own people would realize that God was using him to rescue them, but they did not." This was his moment of self-actualization. He thought his people would connect the dots and realize he was their deliverer, but they did not. Now, he had blood on his hands.

The very next day, he went again to see his people to try once more. This time he saw two Hebrews fighting. Acts 7:23 says, "…He tried to reconcile them by saying, 'Men, you are brothers; why do you want to hurt each other?'" Again he attempted to position himself as the leader. Their response to his devotional pep talk was, "Who do you think you are? We don't need you or want your help." (Acts 7:27) Moses finally stepped out to identify with his people, but they rejected him.

Exodus 2:15a says, "When Pharaoh heard of this, he tried to kill Moses, but Moses fled from Pharaoh and went to live in Midian…" At forty, the prime of his life, he made a bold leap to make it happen. He put all his relational capital on the line, but came up short. Now, no one wanted Moses. He became a fugitive. The prince of Egypt was a murderer, and a failure.

When Moses stepped on the stage and took a risk, no one wanted to follow. Someone said if you think you're a leader and no one follows, you're only going for a walk. Moses went on a really long walk by himself. In one day, he lost everything—home, career and dream. But, God would give him another chance. Past failures do not disqualify us, but equip us for future ministry. God can redeem the loss and turn it into a lesson we can share with others. Moses' failure would be the area of his future success. Our worst failures are never final.

We must be careful in our judgement on those who seem beyond hope. We should never label anyone a "lost cause." Romans 11:33 says, "Oh, the depth of the riches of the wisdom and knowledge of God! How unsearchable his judgments, and his paths beyond tracing out!" What looks like a career-ending mistake can become part of God's story of redemption.

Truth #3–God loves misfits.

We know that because Jesus was one. His brothers and sisters thought he was crazy (Mark 3:21). Jesus was the wild child. Isaiah 53:3 says of Jesus, "He was despised and rejected by mankind, a man of suffering, and familiar with pain. Like one from whom people hide their faces he was despised, and we held him in low esteem." He was the ultimate misfit, the perfect son of God clothed in flesh and blood, surrounded by sinful people who wanted nothing to do with him. John 1:11 says, "He came unto his own, and his own received him not." He lived on the outside looking in, because his own people did not receive him. But nothing compares to the rejection he felt on the cross when he cried, "My God! My God! Why have you forsaken me?"

Remember this. Jesus was forsaken so you could be accepted forever. He was cursed so you could be blessed. He was rejected so you could be adopted. In Christ there are no misfits, only sons and daughters of God. Romans 5:1 says, "Therefore, since we have been justified through faith, we have peace with God through our Lord Jesus Christ."

Exodus 2:15 says, "…but Moses fled from Pharaoh and went to live in Midian…" Midian was a territory outside of Egyptian control, in the northwest regions of the Arabian Desert. The Midianites traced their heritage back to Midian, a son of Abraham through his wife Keturah, whom he married after the death of Sarah. Possibly it was this family connection that drove Moses to travel there.

It wasn't easy. He spent many days in the searing sun and struggled to sleep in the frigid night air. But one day, off in the distance, he spotted a well. As he sat resting and enjoying a refreshing drink, he saw seven young women approaching to water their flocks. People have lived in the Arabian Desert for thousands of years. It is a nomadic life, revolving around finding water and green pasture for camels, horses and sheep.

As they approached the well, some other roughneck shepherds rolled up. Exodus 2:17 says, "Some shepherds came along and drove them away…" Very likely there were catcalls, hoots, obscene gestures, or even attempts to have their way sexually. It was not a safe situation, because the Bible says in Exodus 2:17, "…Moses got up and came to their rescue and watered their flock." The tired prince still had some fight. After kicking butt Egyptian style, I'm sure the ladies were impressed. Moses went over the top and watered their flocks, probably with a grin and a wink.

Moses did the work in record time because when the girls got back home, their father asked, "Why have you returned so early today?" (Ex. 2:18) That's when they told him about the mysterious Egyptian. The curious and thankful father invited the stranger to stay.

The atmosphere in this wilderness home was much more relaxed than the palace. Zero pressure to perform or impress. There were long meals, walks, and plenty of time for conversation. Jethro grew to like Moses and wanted him to stay so much he offered his daughter Zipporah as a wife.

What a strange wedding that must have been. Zipporah's side had all the family and friends, while Moses stood alone. Soon after, they had their first child. Moses named him Gershom which in the Hebrew sounds like "a foreigner there." Though blessed with a wife, son, and extended family, inside he felt like a foreigner, a misfit living in a strange land.

If you're going through a season of transition, and struggling to find your place, take note of a few lessons from Moses. First, find a family. Let's put ourselves in Jethro's shoes. Out of the bush came a young, powerful, educated man all by his lonesome, 300 hundred miles from home. Everyone was curious about his story, a story he couldn't spin. It was awkward at dinner time for a while.

This wilderness family was a Godsend. They welcomed a mysterious traveler to their table. Before they knew what he believed or what he had done, they accepted him. They gave him space and time to unload his baggage. God wants his church to be like this Midianite family, a place where strangers are welcomed; especially those who are not ready to share their story.

In your wilderness, God will lead you to the right family. You will know you've found the place as soon as you walk in. You will see other misfits, joined together in community, showing hospitality. It might be awkward, but don't go back to the desert. In time, you'll find the courage to open up. You'll be surprised how God takes your story and makes it a message of hope for others.

Second, find a friend. Moses grew up not knowing his dad, but he saw a father figure in Jethro. He was the priest of Midian, a spiritual leader in his community, a strong family man, and a friend of God. He became a life-long mentor to Moses. Practically, Jethro knew how to survive in a dangerous world. He knew how to find water, grow crops and protect his clan. Jethro had a gift of wisdom and discernment.

Finally, find a place to make a difference. Moses didn't sit around like a prince. Exodus 3:1 says, "Now Moses was tending the flock of Jethro his father-in-law, the priest of Midian…" Egyptians saw shepherds as nomadic, shady, uncivilized, and untrustworthy (Genesis 46:34). No Egyptian worth his salt aspired to be a shepherd. But Moses saw a need, even though it was well below his training, experience and ability. In a stunning plot twist, the prince of Egypt put down his scepter, and picked up a staff.

With nothing but time on his hands, he took the job of caring for what belonged to someone else. Slowly this natural born leader, with a forceful personality learned to put the needs of the flock ahead of himself. He developed the patience to guide the herd at speeds they could manage.

In time, mighty Moses developed a heart of compassion. He also became an expert at wilderness survival, reading the skies, predicting the weather, and most importantly, finding food and water. Through it all, God used the flocks of Jethro to prepare Moses for his future. The heat of the wilderness melted away his pride until he was like clay in God's hands.

In the season of transition, let's not wait around for God to send us a major assignment. It's dangerous to sit at home with the blinds pulled, the door locked, and the TV on. Maybe the only place to serve is an area far beneath your level of experience. They just need you to show up, set up, tear down, and do it with a smile.

Matthew Henry put it this way, "Let those that think themselves buried alive be content to shine like lamps in their sepulchers and wait till God's time comes for setting them on a candlestick." One day, as he led the sheep, God brought Moses to a burning bush and his life's calling. 1 Peter 4:10 says, "Each of you should use whatever gift you have received to serve others, as faithful stewards of God's grace in its various forms."

4

The Call of Moses

But he said to me, "My grace is sufficient
for you, for my power is made perfect
in weakness." (2 Corinthians 12:9)

As Moses resigned himself to shepherding on the backside of the desert, I don't think his self-talk was very affirming. It probably went something like this, "I could have made something of my life. It's too late now. I failed and everyone knows. I must be a failure." In time, he lost his mojo, charisma, and gift of gab. According to Acts 7:22, as a young stud in Pharaoh's court, he was "mighty in words and deeds." But after spending so much time in the wilderness, he desperately needed a Toastmaster's Club. Mighty Moses struggled daily with the inner giants of inferiority and shame.

In David A Seamands' helpful book *Healing for Damaged Emotions*, he writes, "Satan's greatest psychological weapon is a gut-level feeling of inferiority, inadequacy, and low self-worth. This feeling shackles many Christians, despite wonderful spiritual experiences, despite their faith and knowledge of God's Word…they are tied up in knots, bound by terrible feelings of…worthlessness." He goes on to give four ways inferiority shatters our lives—by paralyzing potential, destroying dreams, ruining relationships, and sabotaging our Christian service.

We find references to Moses' age in a sermon by Stephen in Acts 7. Acts 7:23 says, "When Moses was forty years old, he decided to visit his own people, the Israelites." At age forty, in the prime of life, he fled Egypt. Then in Acts 7:30 we read, "Now when forty years had passed, an angel appeared to him in the wilderness of Mount Sinai, in a flame of fire in a bush." So, it took Moses 80 years to find his calling. He wasn't just over the hill; he fully out to pasture, and yet he continued to show up. One day he found himself at Mount Horeb, also known as Mount Sinai. Today, the locals in this region of Egypt call it Jabal Musa, or the "Mountain of Moses."

While tending to his duties, Moses saw a bush on fire, which was not an uncommon site. Dry shrubs burst into flames often on the hot desert floor. But while this bush burned, it was not consumed. In Exodus 3:3 Moses said, "I will turn aside to see this great sight..." Even at eighty, the old fart was still hungry. Instead of keeping to his routine, he made a choice to investigate. That small decision to follow an inner prodding changed his life.

Notice verse 4, "When the Lord saw that he turned aside to see, God called to him out of the bush, 'Moses, Moses!'" Observe the personal nature of God. He knows our names. He is familiar with all our ways. Psalm 139:7 says, "Where can I go from your Spirit? Where can I flee from your presence?" While he might have felt abandoned, Moses was never forgotten by God.

In Exodus 3:5 God said, "Do not come near; take your sandals off your feet, for the place on which you are standing is holy ground." It was an Egyptian custom to remove sandals before entering a temple to keep dirt and filth out. This was a gesture of respect, a physical act symbolizing an attitude of the heart. In reverence, Moses wanted to remove any impurity and sin in order to have personal contact with a holy God.

As he bowed his face to the ground, God spoke. It was time to rescue his people and give them a home of their own. In this land of abundance, their livestock would produce rich milk, and the ground would yield crops as sweet as honey. Then, in Exodus 3:9 God said, "So now, go. I am sending you to Pharaoh to bring my people the Israelites out of Egypt."

Forty years before, he was itching for a chance to be the hero. Now, he had to be drawn out of hiding. In this holy moment with God, Moses shared his fears, doubts and insecurities. For every question God had an answer.

Truth #4—God can fill our inadequacy with his sufficiency.

Notice Moses' response in Exodus 3:11, "Who am I that I should go to Pharaoh and bring the Israelites out of Egypt?" Here's the first question, "Who am I that I should go?" He was saying, "You're 40 years too late. I had my chance and failed." Instead of failure being an event, it had become his identity.

Inadequacy comes from the Latin *adaequatus* which means "made equal to." When you're *in-adaequatus* you don't feel equal to the task, or to other people. In reality Moses had everything he needed—talent, energy, training, and smarts. But he no longer identified these God-given qualities in himself.

In response, God said in Exodus 3:12, "I will be with you..." God was saying, "Get your eyes off yourself, and your yesterday. Focus on me. You can because I can, and I will be with you."

The other day our dryer suddenly stopped working. All the signs pointed to a blown breaker. I decided to try and fix it myself. After doing some YouTube research, I turned off the power to the house, removed the breaker panel, and unscrewed some wires. That's when I paused. I pictured my eyeballs blowing up like in Raiders of the Lost Ark. So I phoned an electrician friend from church. He marched in with a tool belt and the all-important volt meter, and relieved all my fears. Moses spent a lot of time by himself counting sheep. But God said, "You're not alone. We'll do this together."

Still Moses had more questions to work through. In Exodus 3:13 he said, "If I come to the people of Israel and say to them, 'The God of your fathers has sent me to you,' and they ask me, 'What is his name?' what shall I say to them?" Here was the second question: "Who are you? What kind of God are you?" In ancient Israel, a person's name gave insight into their character and reputation. Moses wanted a deeper understanding of God's nature.

The most common names for God in the Old Testament are *Elohim* and *Yahweh*. *Elohim*, translated as "God," communicates transcendence, supremacy, otherness, and omnipotence. The name *Yahweh*, translated "Lord," is the personal name for God. As the Lord, he owns, provides, sustains, and graciously attends and cares for everything he's made.

From the end of Genesis up to this point in Exodus only the name *Elohim* is used. But in Exodus 3, for the first time, the name *Yahweh* appears. This gives us an insight into the spiritual condition of the Israelites and Moses. They knew God as distant and remote, but while in Egypt they had forgotten the Lord, who is caring, compassionate, and faithful.

So, Moses asked, "Who are you? What is your name?" And, God answered in Exodus 3:14, "I AM WHO I AM...Say this to the people of Israel: I AM has sent me to you." What an interesting name–I AM WHO I AM.

The Hebrew word for "I AM" is *hayah*. It is a verb, a form of speech expressing action. The Hebrew tense for *hayah* in Exodus 3:14 is the imperfect, which communicates not only present but future action. It means not only I AM WHO I AM, but I WILL BE WHO I WILL BE. Also, *hayah* is the root word for *Yahweh*. More than a moniker, God gave Moses deeper insight into his character.

In a world of disruptive change, the Lord never changes. He is the same yesterday, today and forever. He is always faithful. He is also a

God of action. He is involved in the present fulfilling his promises, and will do the same in the future. Yet, He is pre-existent. No one dreamed up the idea of God. He has no beginning and no end. Like the burning bush that never died, our God is a self-sustaining, all-consuming fire. He is not dependent on anyone. There is no end to his resources. He is the Lord of all. He is omnipotent.

If Moses needed a bucket, God was ready with an ocean. While people wonder when the world will stop turning, and how long the sun will keep burning, our Lord holds the universe in his hand. Even more, he hears, knows, and cares. To summarize, the Lord is all-sufficient, omniscient, omnipresent, omnipotent, pre-existent, independent, yet compassionate, faithful, and full of love. As followers of Jesus, we should remember the name *Yahweh* was given to our Savior. Jesus Christ is Lord!

What we see as limitations are opportunities for an all-sufficient God. Let's stop fixating on what we don't have, and put our faith in the I AM. In 2 Corinthians 9:8, Paul says, "And God is able to make all grace abound to you, so that having all sufficiency in all things at all times, you may abound in every good work."

Still, Moses couldn't see his little old self being used in this way. In Exodus 4:1 he continued, "But behold, they will not believe me or listen to my voice, for they will say, 'The Lord did not appear to you.'" Here is the third question: "What if I fail again?" As little kids, failure was part of our everyday learning experience. If we fell from the monkey bars we dusted ourselves off and tried again. As we age, we become risk-averse and fall prey to "life-paralysis." We watch the opportunities of life pass by because we're too afraid to make another mistake.

God graciously gave Moses two signs to perform. First, God told him to throw down his shepherd's staff. Exodus 4:3 says, "…So he threw it on the ground, and it became a serpent, and Moses ran from it." A snake was not a new sight for Moses, so this one must have been large and aggressive, because he ran.

Moses was also running from God's call out of fear. Going back to Egypt was as scary as grabbing a snake by the tail. But God said in Exodus 4:3, "Put out your hand and catch it by the tail…" He was going to have to run at his fear with both hands. So timid Moses started for the snake. When he got ahold of the tail it turned stiff as a stick and became a useful instrument in his hand. The thing we fear most can become a useful instrument if we will run after it with faith and grab hold. The greatest fears in life are most often areas of incredible opportunity.

I met a talented mom serving at church the other Sunday. She works at a family friendly comedy club doing improv, much like the TV show *Who's Line Is It Anyway?* I asked her, "How do you do that? How did you learn to get on a stage in front of crowds and improv?" She said, "I tell people you have to take a step of faith. Once you step out into the unknown everything else falls in place."

Next, God told Moses to put his hand in his cloak. When he pulled it out it was white with leprosy, the kiss of death in the ancient world. At God's command he put his hand back inside, and when he removed it his hand was restored. For every incurable situation God has the answer. In the dead ends of life he is our new beginning. God was about to do a work of resurrection for Moses and Israel. Moses had everything he needed—his staff, cloak, and the call of God.

Still Moses was hesitant and afraid. Calling out from his pit of despair he said in Exodus 4:10, "Oh, my Lord, I am not eloquent, either in the past or since you have spoken to your servant, but I am slow of speech and of tongue." The Bible never explicitly states that Moses stuttered, but he had all the signs.

There is a well known joke about Moses' speech impediment. God came to Moses and asked him to pick a land for the Israelites to inhabit. Somehow Moses knew Canada was rich in natural resources, including oil, and so he tried to say Canada. But when he stammered,

"Can...Can...Can...Can..." God thought he was saying Canaan, and gave him what we know as Israel today.

Those who stammer are often terrified of speaking, and always look for a spokesperson. There is persistent avoidance and hesitation. Stuttering and stammering can become a condition later in life because of intense trauma, stress, anxiety, grief, and loss.

In response, God said in Exodus 4:11, "Who gave human beings their mouths? Who makes them deaf or mute? Who gives them sight or makes them blind? Is it not I, the Lord?" God was saying, "More than feeling adequate, I just need you to be available." Moses already had the skills to speak, they were just rusty. He had been sitting around thinking too much.

If you wait until you're fully prepared you will never do anything. You don't need to take a nightly course at the community college on oral communications. Many dreams get stuck in the planning and preparation phase. We have reams of research but no results. So, we aim, aim, aim, but never fire. General George S. Patton once said, "A good plan violently executed today is better than a perfect plan tomorrow."

Moses gave up sharing his fears, and just downright refused to go. He said in Exodus 4:13, "Pardon your servant, Lord. Please send someone else." Why would God ever call such a hesitant, fearful, self-doubting person? To help Moses get off his dime, God stirred the heart of his brother Aaron. After a visible manifestation of God's presence, the signs and wonders, the audible voice of God, even Moses needed a compadre. Exodus 4:14 says, "...Is there not Aaron, your brother, the Levite? I know that he can speak well. Behold, he is coming out to meet you, and when he sees you, he will be glad in his heart."

What a reunion in the wilderness. The lost brother he never met, came looking for him in the desert, eager to join him in the mission. Finally, a ray of hope broke through the darkness. Moses turned from the wilderness and set his sights on returning home and fulfilling God's call.

In her book *The Gifts of Imperfection*, Brené Brown writes this about shame. "Shame needs three things to grow out of control in our lives: secrecy, silence, and judgment. When something shaming happens, and we keep it locked up, it festers and grows. It consumes us. We need to share our experience…If we can find someone who has earned the right to hear our story, we need to tell it. Shame loses power when it is spoken."

More than anyone, Jesus has earned the right to hear our story of shame. In Exodus 3 and 4 Moses opened up the dark closet of his heart. In the same way, we can draw near to Jesus any hour of the day. Each time we do, shame and inadequacy lose their power.

If you don't feel like you measure up, turn to Ephesians chapter one and get your mind around what God says about you. You are chosen, blessed, holy, blameless, loved, adopted, redeemed, forgiven, included, sealed with the Holy Spirit, empowered by his incomparably great power, made alive, raised up with Christ, seated with him in the heavenly realms, saved by grace, and God's workmanship created for good works (Ephesians 1-2). You are who God says you are.

What is your reason for not responding to the call of God? Why do you keep putting it off? Is it because you feel unworthy? The message of shame blares in your head, "I'm not enough. I don't have enough. What if I fail? I can't speak. I can't organize. I can't manage. I can't live the Christian life. I can't do this or that. I can't. I can't. I can't." Begin to say, "By God's grace I can and I will." Let's get over what you can't do.

Remember who is with you—Jesus Christ the Lord, the all-sufficient one. To drive this point home Jesus took the "I AM WHO I AM" name revealed to Moses and applied it to himself. He said in John 8:58, "Truly, truly, I say to you, before Abraham was, I AM." As Lord, he can fill your inadequacy with his sufficiency.

It's time for a decision. Our English word "decision" comes from the Latin *decidere*, which means "to cut off." You have to make a break with the past to chart a new course. It's time for an incision. It's time to cut the ropes and let the hot air balloon of your faith rise from the ground. Make a decision to follow the Lord.

God isn't through with you. He is calling today, "Let's try again." In 2 Corinthians 9:8 Paul writes, "God can pour on the blessings in astonishing ways so that you're ready for anything and everything, more than just ready to do what needs to be done."

SEASON 2

The Testing Season

5

Breaking Through Barriers

"With your help I can advance against a troop;
with my God I can scale a wall." (Psalm 18:29)

In the movie *Cast Away*, Tom Hanks plays Chuck Noland, a type-A logistics bigwig for FedEx. He's obsessed with time, efficiency, and tasks. After receiving an emergency call on Christmas Eve, he rushed to the airport with his beloved fiancé, and promised to return shortly. But the plane hit a deadly storm, and crashed into the ocean. Busy Chuck found himself stranded on a deserted island.

In the first few weeks, he was determined to survive and escape. He took scattered driftwood and spelled the word "HELP" on the sand. He found a pair of ice skates in a washed up package and used the blades to crack open coconuts for water. He scoured the island in search for inhabitants.

Then one day he saw a light far out in the ocean, and decided to make a break for it. Using a damaged, half inflated raft, he paddled vigorously out to sea. But pounding surf created a ferocious barrier around the island. The harder he paddled the higher the waves rose, and the struggling raft was soon upended. Gasping for air, another surge crashed on his head. Tumbling underwater a jagged piece of coral pierced his leg. He limped back to shore, convinced he would never escape. To keep his sanity, he developed an imaginary friend, a washed up volleyball. With blood from his wounds, he painted a face on the ball and named him "Wilson."

In the next segment, the words, "Four years later…" appear on the screen. Chuck has changed. He looks like Moses, long beard, scraggly hair, skin tanned and leather-like. The unknown island had become a familiar land. He learned how to hunt and find water. One day, while squatting and gnawing on a piece of raw fish pulled from his homemade spear, a large corner section of a Don's Jon washed up. An idea was born. He could try using the plastic wall as a sail. As Wilson looked on, he set to work building a large wooden raft, tying the pieces together with vines.

There was no turning back. Waiting for change was no longer an option. Plunging the raft into the sea, he paddled with desperation. At just the right moment, he raised his plastic sail and broke through the last barrier into the wild ocean.

In that moment, Chuck looked back at the lonely island that had been his home for the last four years as if to say goodbye. In a strange way, his heart longed for what had become familiar. But he knew he wasn't made to live in isolation, scavenging for food. The decision to lay it all on the line saved his life.

What we see in Moses and Chuck Noland is a comeback. I believe God wants that for each of us. I don't know what you've been through, how many times you've failed, or how old you are. God has a comeback season for you. To get to that place you'll have to say goodbye to the island, the wilderness, the site of sadness, the comfortable place of your languishing.

Truth #5—For every barrier, God has a breakthrough.

As Moses launched into a new season, he had three different barriers standing in his way. The first barrier was adversity in marriage.

Exodus 4:20 says, "So Moses took his wife and sons, put them on a donkey and started back to Egypt. And he took the staff of God in his hand." The Bible is silent on how Zipporah felt about the transition, but we learn a lot from her actions. Big moves are always tough. Following this wild dream meant saying goodbye to her childhood home, her loving father, and her extended family. This was no vacation, but a donkey ride across the desert.

We all know Moses was not a big talker. He admitted at the burning bush, "I am slow of tongue." Zipporah could probably tie him up in linguistic knots before he got a word out. As they traveled with nothing but time to spend together, there wasn't much communication, especially about one huge, contentious issue.

It had to do with the sacred rite of circumcision for infant males, the outward sign commanded by God to show covenant relationship (Genesis 17:10). For some reason, Zipporah didn't want her boys circumcised. Maybe she thought it was cruel and disgusting. Remember, she could water an entire flock of sheep, so she was no wallflower. She put her foot down, and mighty Moses gave in. In a marriage, usually one is a skunk and the other is a turtle. The skunk explodes and stinks up the house. The turtle retreats and hides. But hiding and stinking up the joint only magnifies our problems. Their relationship was at a standstill and they were not working together.

So we read in Exodus 4:24, "At a lodging place on the way, the Lord met Moses and was about to kill him." Apparently God is deadly serious about his commands, especially for those he calls to leadership. Whatever the relational dynamics, God held Moses responsible. How could he be God's lawgiver when his own family didn't keep God's laws? We don't know if Moses came down with leprosy, if he was bit by a viper, or if an angel stood ready to strike him with a flaming sword. The Lord was just about to kill Moses when Zipporah acquiesced. Exodus 4:25-26 says, "But Zipporah took a flint knife, cut off her son's foreskin and touched Moses' feet with it. (She said) 'Surely you are a bridegroom of blood to me...'"

Like Moses, the great evangelist and founder of the Methodist Church, John Wesley, had major marriage issues. He was an austere, spiritual giant, consumed with work. But his wife Mary grew to hate the silence and neglect. In time she became angry, jealous, and controlling. One Methodist preacher, named John Hampson, said he once entered a room and found Mary pulling John Wesley on the floor by his hair. In her hands were locks of his hair she had pulled up by the roots.

As we go after God's call, our bedrooms can become battlegrounds. While fighting devils outside, all hell breaks loose in the home. Marriage is the union of two imperfect people with different personalities, preferences, abilities, and weaknesses. When our differences come to live under one roof there will be conflict.

The keys to breaking through this barrier are forgiveness and heartfelt communication. When conflicts rise don't allow the offense to fester and become a bitter wound. When wounded, we build up protective walls to isolate ourselves and punish the offender. We shut off communication, the lifeblood of any relationship. Inflamed with anger we believe we're sleeping with the enemy.

My dad's side of the family hails from wild and woolly West Virginia, the rugged mountaineer state. Grandpa Whitlow and dad had a unique sound they often made when communicating with one another. It sounded like "eeeeyuh." Grandpa would look at dad and say, "eeeyuh" and dad would reply a few seconds later, "eeeeyuh." They would then smile at each other knowing everything was OK.

Your spouse deserves more than a "eeeyuh." Instead of a grunt and scratch, get close. Look at each other in the eyes, and share your thoughts and feelings. Don't let the sun go down on your anger. Forgive one another and flush out any offenses so that nothing hinders your communication. Ephesians 4:32 says, "Be kind and compassionate to one another, forgiving each other, just as in Christ God forgave you."

The second barrier Moses faced was unmet expectations. After arriving in Egypt, he and Aaron gathered the people, shared God's plan to free them, and performed the miracles. They believed the message, and bowed their heads in thankful worship. Buoyed by the response, Moses finally stood before Pharaoh. Much had changed in forty years. The former prince of Egypt, turned fugitive and wilderness shepherd, stood in the palace again. The castaway had come back.

Moses started off with a small request. Notice Exodus 5:1, "This is what the Lord, the God of Israel, says: 'Let my people go, so that they may hold a festival to me in the wilderness.'" Instead of asking for full release, Mosses requested a few days off to hold a festival. He was testing the waters, to soften Pharaoh's heart.

But notice Pharaoh's response in Exodus 5:2, "Who is the Lord, that I should obey him and let Israel go? I do not know the Lord and I will not let Israel go." Of the many deities worshipped in Egypt, Pharaoh was at the top, believed to be the son of Ra, god of the sun. He would never stoop and submit to the foreign deity of his slaves. In Exodus 5:3 Moses continued to press, "The God of the Hebrews has met with us. Now let us take a three-day journey into the wilderness to offer sacrifices to the Lord our God..."

I can just picture a long awkward pause as Pharaoh and Moses stared at one another, like two cowboys about to draw. Then Pharaoh said in Exodus 5:4, "Moses and Aaron, why are you taking the people away from their labor?" Pharaoh turned the tables and made Moses the problem, claiming he was taking the people from their work, selling them a hopeless fantasy. To destroy any faith in Moses, he punished the Israelites by confiscating their complimentary straw for making bricks. The tired slaves had to scour the land for every scrap while their quota of bricks stayed the same. When they fell short they were mocked and beaten without mercy. The dispirited overseers found

Moses and blamed him for the horrible turn of events. In Exodus 5:21 we read their accusations, "May the Lord look on you and judge you! You have made us obnoxious to Pharaoh and his officials and have put a sword in their hand to kill us."

"May the Lord look on you and judge you," was tantamount to pronouncing a curse on Moses. I'm sure he expected a different outcome. He had no idea while standing in the court of Pharaoh that he was right in the center of a spiritual battlefield. Satan knew God's plan to bless the children of Israel so they could bless the world and bring salvation through the seed of Abraham, Jesus the Messiah. Pharaoh was his agent to defy and destroy God's people.

We're in the same battle. Ephesians 6:12 says, "For our struggle is not against flesh and blood, but against the rulers, against the authorities, against the powers of this dark world and against the spiritual forces of evil in the heavenly realms." Much of the strife in our life is a manifestation of the real battle in the spiritual realm. We're called by God to lead our children, friends, and family to Jesus so they can experience salvation and eternal life. But the enemy's mission is to thwart that plan. The devil will not go down without a fight. When we step out in faith, and things get worse, let's not be surprised.

Bringing the sacrifice of praise is a powerful way to overcome our adversary's opposition and break through the disappointment of unmet expectations. It's a sacrifice because we put to death that part of us that wants to gripe and complain. Even though we don't feel like it, we give to God an offering with the fruit of our lips.

The purpose of your life is to glorify God. In fact, your body is like a musical instrument. You have pipes, vocal cords, chambers for resonance, bags full of air, and a unique heartbeat. When we use this instrument to praise, God does for us what we could never do ourselves. He fights our battles and fills our hearts with joy.

In the book *Make Your Bed*, US Navy Admiral Bill McRaven shares a memory from his time in Seal training. The most challenging part of Seal training is "Hell Week," a six-day period of no sleep, mental harassment, and continual physical exercise. On Wednesday of Hell Week, McRaven and the others paddled their rafts to the Mud Flats between San Diego and Tijuana, where there are large patches of thick, swampy, earthy sludge. They spent the entire evening and night in the freezing mud trying to survive. Within the first hour, each man was mired in muck, covered from head to toe.

On this most challenging night, because of some violation, Admiral McRaven and his team were forced to spend more time in the mud. Clothed in brown slime, the whites of their eyes shown in the night. With the wind howling, the instructor spoke through a bullhorn. They could leave and head for a warm fire if just five would give up. If only five would quit, they all could escape the icy mud and wicked wind. As they all sat and contemplated their fate, some were ready to throw in the towel. Admiral McRaven writes what happened next.

"The chattering teeth and shivering moans of the trainees were so loud it was hard to hear anything and then, one voice began to echo through the night—one voice raised in song. The song was terribly out of tune, but sung with great enthusiasm. One voice became two and two became three and before long everyone in the class was singing. We knew that if one man could rise above the misery then others could as well.

The instructors threatened us with more time in the mud if we kept up the singing—but the singing persisted. And somehow—the mud seemed a little warmer, the wind a little tamer and the dawn not so far away."

Our weapon is not a sword but a song. The walls of Jericho came crashing down after a shout of praise (Joshua 6). At God's command, Jehoshaphat sent the choir ahead of the army to give thanks (2 Chronicles 20). As they praised, the invaders turned on one another in confusion. As Paul and Silas praised, God shook the doors of their prison and set them free (Acts 16). Like Superman hates Kryptonite, our adversary, the devil, is allergic to our praise.

The third barrier Moses faced was rejection and despair. After failing with Pharaoh, Moses said to the Lord in Exodus 5:22-23, "Why, Lord, why have you brought trouble on this people? Is this why you sent me?" God graciously spoke to him again, communicated the vision, and encouraged him to go to the people once more. He went as commanded. But the ears of the Israelites were blocked with discouragement (Exodus 6:9). Moses was just another fake prophet singing a silly song.

Rejected by Pharaoh and the people once again, Moses laid bare his soul in Exodus 6:12, "If the Israelites will not listen to me, why would Pharaoh listen to me, since I speak with faltering lips?" Still, the Lord continued to tell Moses all he promised to do in Egypt. But in Exodus 6:30 Moses said the same old thing, "Since I speak with faltering lips, why would Pharaoh listen to me?"

Even after the burning bush, Moses still battled with relentless uncertainty and insecurity. "I can't speak. Why would Pharaoh listen to me? No one wants to follow me." Just like Moses, we talk about ourselves throughout the day. Research tells us about 80 percent of our daily self-talk is negative. Just imagine a drill sergeant following you around all day long yelling in your ear, telling you how awful you are. We say things about ourselves we would never say to anyone else.

To break through this barrier we can renew our minds with God's Word. Peter writes in 1 Peter 1:23, "For you have been born again, not of perishable seed, but of imperishable, through the living and enduring word of God." Notice the Bible described as an indestructible, life-giving seed. Our minds are like a garden, and every thought we dwell on is a seed. After a failure or two, our garden gets overgrown with the weeds, thistles, and thorns of negativity.

I once was very discouraged with the crab grass in our front yard. Every time I pulled a little up, it only caused more to grow. Bewildered,

I called a lawn specialist. He said the best way to get rid of bad grass is to plant new grass seed. In time, the good grass will take root, leaving no room for the bad grass to grow. Much like this, every time we read, meditate, and memorize God's Word we are sowing good seed.

One of the greatest hymn writers of the church was Fanny Crosby. She was born March 24, 1820, just outside New York City. Fanny suffered a horrible loss when she was just 6 months old. She came down with a stubborn eye infection. Because their regular doctor was out of town, her worried parents found another physician they didn't know. He told them to place hot mustard compresses on her eyes. The doctor, they later discovered, was a fake, and his prescription caused Fanny to lose her sight. The quack doctor skipped town and was never seen again.

Fanny came from a family of devoted Christians, who loved the Bible. Her grandmother helped her memorize Scripture when she was around ten years old. Her mind was a sponge, soaking up five chapters a week. By the age of 15, she had memorized Genesis, Exodus, Leviticus, Numbers, Deuteronomy, some of the Psalms, Proverbs, Song of Solomon, Matthew, Mark, Luke, and John.

Strengthened by God's promises, she refused to wallow in despair. We see this in one of her first poems composed when she was only eight.

> Oh what a happy soul I am, although I cannot see;
> I am resolved that in this world contented I will
> be. How many blessings I enjoy, that other people
> don't; To weep and sigh because I'm blind, I cannot,
> and I won't.

In her career she composed over 8,000 hymns. Many of her songs are widely sung today. In her most famous hymn, "Blessed Assurance," Fanny testifies, "This is my story, this is my song, praising my Savior all the day long." And, in "To God be the Glory" she encourages us to

"Praise the Lord! Praise the Lord! Let the earth hear his voice. Praise the Lord! Praise the Lord! Let the people rejoice. O, come to the Father, through Jesus the Son, and give him the glory, great things he has done." Her energy and love for Jesus attracted and inspired many until her death at 95 years of age.

At last, we read in Exodus 7:6-7, "Moses and Aaron did just as the Lord commanded them. Moses was eighty years old and Aaron eighty-three when they spoke to Pharaoh." This was the big breakthrough point in Moses' journey. It took 80 years, but he finally got over himself. Never again do we find him fixated on his speech impediment.

What barriers are you facing today? If your marriage isn't what it could be, hang in there. Continue to show up, giving, forgiving, and communicating. When life doesn't meet expectations, pour out your praise. Plant the good seeds of God's Word in the garden of your mind. For every barrier, there is a breakthrough. God has a comeback season in store for you.

6

He's as Cold as Ice

"Above all else, guard your heart, for everything
you do flows from it." (Psalm 51:17)

B ack in eighth grade, some random person saved my life. In those
days, long walks home from school were common. It was good
for burning the pent-up energy, but it left much unsupervised time to
get in trouble. Every middle schooler had one common desire. We all
wanted to see a fight. When one broke out, the chant began, "Fight!
Fight! Fight!"

In that crazy season of life, a "friend" told me that someone I didn't
know called me a sissy. That didn't bother me until he followed up with,
"What are you going to do about that?" I thought for a moment and
responded, "I don't know. What do you think I should do?" He told
me how the word had spread and that I'd better do something. So, I
said, "Tell him I said take it back." My nemesis refused to take it back.
So I told my bud to try again, but this time add, "I'm really serious."

A silly game of back and forth escalated throughout the day. I don't
know what I was thinking. I was a skinny preacher's kid who played
the trumpet beside grandma's organ. My opponent was stocky, with
linebacker shoulders, and thick biceps. Caught up in the hype and
attention, I walked out of school ready to defend my honor.

A crowd of students gathered around us as we walked toward an open playground. People I had never met patted me on the back, wishing me luck. Then everyone stopped and created a large circle around us. I pumped my fists and pranced around like Rocky. But in just a few seconds, he had me pinned to the dirt. His heavy knees were on my shoulders. It felt like a grown man was sitting on my stomach. The only thing I knew to do was cover my face with my hands to shield it from the pounding that was sure to come.

Right when I thought I was dead, the suffocating weight was lifted off me. I uncovered my face and saw the bottoms of his soles being drug away. To this day, I don't know how or why. Some loving, influential soul in that depraved group of humanity had mercy on me.

The tired, discouraged Hebrew slaves were in no condition to fight Pharaoh and the world class Egyptian army. When they were unable to save themselves, God stepped in and fought for his people. They were rescued from slavery, not through any works of their own, but by the mighty hand of God.

Our English word "plague" comes from the Greek word *plaga*, which means "to strike." The Egyptian taskmasters struck the exposed backs of their Hebrew slaves. The Israelite foremen were beaten for not meeting their quota of bricks. In the ten plagues, God struck back and brought the most sophisticated nation in the ancient world to its knees.

Over and over again, God commanded Pharaoh, "Let my people go." I don't know why God wanted Israel to be his people. They didn't have much to offer. The only explanation is love. When no one wanted them God said, "I want them to be my people."

As you look back, aren't you thankful for the goodness and mercy of God? The Apostle Paul put it this way in Ephesians 2:4-5, "But because of his great love for us, God, who is rich in mercy, made us alive with Christ even when we were dead in transgressions—it is by grace you have been saved."

Scholars see a pattern in the plague narratives found in Exodus 7-10. The first nine are usually grouped together because they increase in severity and lead to the final blow that set Israel free. Also, the first nine are organized in three groups of three because the first, fourth, and seventh plagues each begin with Moses confronting Pharaoh early in the morning.

In our modern age, many see the plagues as just another example of a harsh, cruel, angry God. Let's remember, God graciously gave the wicked king ample warnings. And at the start of every new plague cycle, Pharaoh had a face-to-face, early morning appointment with God's prophet. But each time God spoke, Pharaoh resisted. (Exodus 7:13, 7:22, 7:15, 8:32, 9:7, 9:12, 9:35, 10:20, 10:27). With every "no" another callused layer was placed over his heart. The gradual hardening of his heart teaches us our next lesson.

Truth #6–Every time we tell God "no" the colder our hearts will grow.

God sent Moses and Aaron to Pharaoh with the command to let his people go. Pharaoh asked for a sign, and Aaron's staff turned into a snake. The king's magicians were able to do the same with their "secret arts." But Aaron's snake quickly devoured their serpents. The serpent was their symbol of power and authority. It was the featured emblem on Pharaoh's headpiece. But Exodus 7:13 says, "Yet Pharaoh's heart became hard and he would not listen…"

Cycle 1

Moses and Aaron confronted Pharaoh early in the morning on the banks of the Nile. He went there to pray and worship. To the Egyptians, the Nile River was not just a body of water, but the physical manifestation of a god. When its banks flooded each year, it left behind beautiful black soil for planting crops. It was the wellspring of their civilization in the middle of the desert, providing water, food, and beauty.

While Pharaoh watched, Aaron struck the river, and it turned to blood. All the fish died, releasing a horrible odor throughout the land. Pharaoh's magicians were able to duplicate the miracle, but this was of no help. Exodus 7:23 says that Pharaoh, "...turned and went into his palace, and did not take even this to heart."

God waited for seven long days. With no response, he sent the frogs. The frog was the manifestation of Heqet, the fertility goddess. Instead of blessing the people, frogs filled every home in Egypt. Can you imagine the noise at night as those toads belched into the morning hours?

Again, the magicians were able to do the same with their "secret arts" but could do nothing to fix the issue. To everyone's surprise, Pharaoh asked for prayer and promised to let the Israelites go. Moses interceded, and the frogs croaked. The people piled the critters in heaps throughout the land. But seeing relief, Pharaoh hardened his heart again and refused to listen.

Then, God told Moses to tell Aaron to strike the ground with his rod. When he did, the New International Version says the dust of the land turned to gnats. The King James Version, however, says the dust turned to lice. The Hebrew word *ken* is not clear, and could be defined either way. We do know the Egyptians were obsessed with cleanliness and order. Imagine the horror a lice infestation would have created. This was the first miracle the magicians were unable to duplicate. Outdone, they went to Pharaoh and said in Exodus 8:19, "This is the finger of God." But Pharaoh's heart was hard and he would not listen.

Cycle 2

As with the start of Cycle 1, Moses met Pharaoh at the break of a new day. Notice God's command in Exodus 8:20, "Get up early in the morning and confront Pharaoh as he goes to the river..." Even after the Nile turned to blood, stubborn Pharaoh kept coming to its stinky shores to pray. So next God promised a scourge of flies. For the first time, Pharaoh heard Goshen would be plague-free.

The winged nuisances filled every home. They ruined everything. The king called for Moses and attempted a compromise. Just sacrifice within the land, and all would be well. But Moses would not settle for less than God commanded. Pharaoh complied. But when relief came, he went back on his word and hardened his heart again.

In plague five, God increased the intensity by striking the livestock with a deadly disease. Hathor, the great mother goddess of the sun god Ra, was depicted as a cow. Where was Hathor now? The symbol of her strength lay lifeless on the ground. This time, Pharaoh left to investigate Goshen and found every animal well fed and at rest. But Exodus 9:7 says, "...Yet his heart was unyielding and he would not let the people go."

Next, God told Moses to take soot from a furnace and throw it in the air. Probably this was a furnace much like the slaves used to make Pharaoh's bricks. The grit blew through the land and caused a plague of festering, puss-filled boils. The magicians that tried to go toe-to-toe with Moses were now stricken so severely they could not even stand.

Cycle 3

Once more, God sent Moses to confront Pharaoh early in the morning. Still, he refused to yield. So Moses lifted his hands. Giant chunks of hail struck the earth with such force they stripped the trees of their branches. The storm crushed the crops and anything living in the fields. It was the worst storm in Egypt's history. Pharaoh confessed, "I have sinned." Moses prayed, but when the thunder stopped, the Egyptian ruler sinned again and hardened his heart.

Before the eighth plague, Moses and Aaron visited Pharaoh and asked, "How long will you refuse to humble yourself?" Pharaoh was dug in like an old tick on a dog. This time, even Pharaoh's officials sided with Moses, "Do you not realize all of Egypt is ruined?" (Exodus 10:7). He tried again to control the outcome and broker a compromise on his terms. They could go and sacrifice, but just leave the women and children behind. When Moses refused, they were driven from Pharaoh's presence.

Like a hungry, invading army, locusts filled the land and devoured everything in sight. Pharaoh quickly called for Moses and pleaded, "Forgive my sin and pray for me once more!" Predictably, when a wind carried the bugs away, he hardened his heart again.

Then, Moses stretched his hand and darkness filled the land. The Bible says the darkness was so thick it was like you could touch it. The great Ra was the sun god, creator of the world, who made the crops grow. Ra traveled in a circuit across the heavens in the day, and down into the underworld at night, only to rise victorious the next morning. In this ninth wonder, their divine light went dark.

Pharaoh attempted to dictate the terms once more. This time, everyone could go except for their flocks and herds. Listen to Moses' response in Exodus 10:26, "...not a hoof is to be left behind." At that, Pharaoh threatened Moses with death if he ever saw his face again.

Heart Exam

Let's pause the story to make some observations. God graciously spoke to Pharaoh through his prophet, but every time, he walked out of the church in the middle of the sermon. So God spoke to him in his circumstances. As his well-ordered world unraveled, everything pointed in a different direction. But he looked the other way. Still, God spoke to him through friends. His closest advisors said, "This is the finger of God." But with every nudge, old Pharaoh bowed his back.

The Bible calls people who will not listen fools. Proverbs 12:15 says, "The way of fools seems right to them, but the wise listen to advice." Not only was Pharaoh a stubborn fool, he was arrogant. He believed he could fight with God and win. In the end, he lost everything.

After plague number six we read something disturbing. Exodus 9:12, "But the Lord hardened the heart of Pharaoh, and he did not listen to them, as the Lord had spoken to Moses." This is repeated after plagues eight, nine, and ten. Which is it? Did Pharaoh harden his own heart or did the Lord?

It's simplistic to say that because Pharaoh was such a stubborn mule, God sped up the hardening process so that he could get what he deserved. Before the plagues, back in Exodus 4:21, God said, "…I will harden his heart so that he will not let the people go."

Here's what we do know. God was in complete control, even of Pharaoh's heart. God said to Pharaoh in Exodus 9:16, "I have raised you up for this very purpose, that I might show you my power and that my name might be proclaimed in all the earth." The proud king's ultimate purpose in life was to be the unforgettable object lesson of God's power, so his fame could spread throughout the world.

When we read how the Lord hardened Pharaoh's heart it creates tension, like a suspended chord in music. We want it to resolve and feel good, but it doesn't. Maybe that's the way God wants it. The tension keeps us at attention, and from taking his grace for granted. Here's the good news. What was true of Pharaoh doesn't have to be true of us. May Psalm 51:10 be our daily prayer, "Create in me a clean heart and renew a right spirit within me."

When we harden our hearts, we put ourselves in God's place. Human beings are blessed with talent, and do many things well. But we make miserable gods. Pharaoh enjoyed the top spot on the long list of Egypt's gods. His most important responsibility was to maintain order, or what Egyptian's called Ma'at. The idea of Ma'at was fundamental. They believed Egypt was the center of the world, and everything around was riddled with disorder and chaos. But mighty Pharaoh sat helpless as the order of Egypt unraveled. Each plague was a psychological blow, exposing his arrogance and frailty.

One of our lesser known founding fathers, Alexander Hamilton, was blessed with amazing gifts and God-given powers. Born out of wedlock in the British West Indies (1755), his father abandoned him when he was ten. Tragically, his mother died a few years later. He started working as a clerk in a warehouse at age 11, and the owners quickly noticed his talents. Some friends got together and sent him to New York to get a proper education at King's College. He arrived just before the American Revolution and distinguished himself in the army, catching the attention of General George Washington. He made young Hamilton a lieutenant colonel and put him in charge of his staff and correspondence. After the war, he wrote the Federalist Papers and worked with James Madison to frame our Constitution. And, when Washington became president, he appointed Hamilton as the first Treasury Secretary.

In his early 30's he sat on top of the world. He had the trust and ear of the president, and was married to an adoring wife named Eliza, who gave birth to their eight children. Many believed he would follow Washington as America's second president. His enemies spread the rumor he secretly aspired to make himself king.

But when he was just 35, his lovely wife took the kids to stay with family in New York. As Hamilton worked from home in Philadelphia, a 23-year-old Maria Reynolds knocked on the door. She asked for financial help claiming her husband had deserted and abused her. He made an appointment for later that evening. When he showed up with the money, she invited him into her bedroom. That began what became the Hamilton Reynolds Affair (1791-1792).

Throughout their year fling, she wrote him many letters begging to see him, and each time, like a lamb to the slaughter he went. With Hamilton trapped in the relationship, Maria's husband, James Reynolds seized the opportunity, and began writing threatening letters. He promised to tell Mrs. Hamilton and the world he if he didn't pay up. Still, he fell for Maria every time she wrote and continued to pay

9

Getting Through the In Betweens

> I was young and now I am old, yet I have
> never seen the righteous forsaken or their
> children begging bread. (Psalm 37:25)

Do you know what the "in betweens" of life are? Here are a few examples. You just bought a new puppy and after months of effort you think he's finally potty-trained. But after a long walk outside he decides to pee on your new couch. Maybe you're in the middle of remodeling, and two by fours, extension chords, and random tools are scattered all over the kitchen. You may be in between jobs. You might be in between sizes—you want to be a 32 but that's still too tight, so you stay in your 42's.

The last chapter was about the greatest salvation miracle in the Old Testament when Pharaoh and his chariot army were swallowed up in the sea. On the other side there was singing, dancing, and shouting. After 430 years the Israelites were free at last.

To celebrate, God led them to a place called Elim (Exodus 15:27). Elim was like a resort in the desert. Here in north Florida there are several state parks with natural springs. The crystal, clear blue water is a cool 72 degrees year around for swimmers to enjoy. Elim had 12 springs. There were seventy palm trees. At this oasis the Israelites hung by the pool and sipped refreshing drinks from coconuts.

But Elim was not the final destination. Notice Exodus 16:1, "The whole Israelite community set out from Elim and came to the Desert of Sin, which is between Elim and Sinai, on the fifteenth day of the second month after they had come out of Egypt."

The retreat at Elim ended and God led them to the Desert of Sin. There is no hidden, spiritual meaning in the name. It was a barren place between Elim and Sinai. Most everyone knows about Sinai – revelation, covenant, breakthrough, the Ten Commandments. Between the oasis of Elim and Sinai, there was desert—a hot, brown, dusty wilderness.

The Israelites were in between. We've all been there. A door closed. A season ended. Something you enjoyed pooped out on you. Someone moved your cheese. Don't think you're strange. Most of life is lived in between Elim and Sinai. We never arrive. There's always a next step, another hill to climb, a problem to solve.

Let's see how they responded. Exodus 16:2-3 says, "In the desert the whole community grumbled against Moses and Aaron. The Israelites said to them, 'If only we had died by the Lord's hand in Egypt! There we sat around pots of meat and ate all the food we wanted, but you have brought us out into this desert to starve this entire assembly to death.'"

As they traveled through the desert, it got so hot the Israelites exploded in a fit of complaining. When we give way to grumbling we can say some crazy things. The Israelites moaned, "In Egypt it was like Texas de Brazil and the Melting Pot. We ate all the food we wanted. Why did we ever leave?"

The Hebrew word for grumble is *loon*. It literally means "to lodge, abide, continue, or dwell." For example, in Ruth 1:16, Ruth said to her mother-in-law Naomi, "For where you go I will go, and where you

lodge (loon) I will lodge (loon)." Grumbling is dwelling on the negative. Psychologists call this a negative explanatory style. We interpret
the events of our life in a gloomy way. That's why the Bible says in
Philippians 2:14, "Do everything without grumbling or arguing." The
house isn't on fire. The ship of life isn't sinking. Lift up your eyes. God
is taking you somewhere

Truth #9–Trust the Provider more than your provisions.

Notice what God said to Moses in Exodus 16:4, "I will rain
down bread from heaven for you…" Bread was an essential part of
the Hebrew diet. It's interesting how we still use bread as a symbol of
provision. We talk about the breadwinner in the home, or our need
for some dough. Jesus had this in mind when he taught his disciples
to pray in Matthew 6:11, "Give us this day our daily bread." In times
of transition our daily bread is a major concern. We all want to get
connected to someone who can make it rain. Only God can make it
rain bread in a desert.

I remember enrolling as a freshman at Oral Roberts University.
The son of a church planter, the only way I got in was through a Pell
Grant. During my first semester dad and mom bought a house, and
I lost all my financial aid. I drove all the way out to Oklahoma from
Virginia to enroll for the second semester, and they said, "You have to
pay thousands of dollars. Sorry."

I called my parents, and they said, "You better pray." With nowhere
else to turn, I went up to my empty dorm room, and prayed for about
four minutes. The last day to enroll finally came. I walked across
campus to the back of the line hoping for a miracle.

Standing there under the hot, Oklahoma sun, a man in a suit
walked up and asked, "Are you Arlie Whitlow?" I said, "Yes." He said,
"Come with me." We walked to the front of the line and sat down at a
computer. After pressing some buttons, he printed a piece of paper out

and said, "Welcome back to ORU." I don't know how, but someone in the administration heard about my need and found me in the back of line. On that day, God made it rain. Philippians 4:19 says, "And my God will meet all your needs according to the riches of his glory in Christ Jesus."

Every need we face is an opportunity for God to express his care and abundant provision. Wherever you are, God cares about your daily bread. In the middle of your wilderness he can make it rain.

In Exodus 16:4-5 God said to Moses, "I will rain down bread from heaven for you. The people are to go out each day and gather enough for that day. In this way I will test them and see whether they will follow my instructions..."

The Hebrew word for "instructions" is *torah,* and means "God's laws." Notice the test had to do with his provision, to see if they could trust and follow his commands. Here was the gist. Gather only enough for each day. No leftovers. On the sixth day, gather twice as much so you can rest and worship on the Sabbath.

Put yourself in their sandals. What if God said to you, "I know there's a problem with the supply chain. But don't go to Costco and hoard all the toilet paper. I'll bring enough provisions each day to your doorstep, like Door Dash. Don't be afraid. Just trust me and follow my instructions. I want to strengthen your faith and show my love for you."

Let's see how the Israelites did. Exodus 16:20 says, "However, some of them paid no attention to Moses; they kept part of it until morning, but it was full of maggots and began to smell. So Moses was angry with them."

They had a mentality of scarcity. Afraid there would not be enough, they paid no attention to God's instructions. The next morning, everything they worked and fretted over was full of maggots. Then on the Sabbath day of rest, they lumbered out to scrounge for something but found nothing. The Lord said to Moses, "How long will you refuse to keep my commands and my instructions?" (Exodus 16:28)

Are you striving to eliminate the needs from your life? If you don't have any needs you don't need God. When our confidence is in our Provider and his promise to supply, it frees us to be generous.

Later in college, dad took me on a mission trip to Haiti. He was invited to train a group of Haitian pastors and dedicate a medical clinic in the interior of the country. During one session, Dad asked if I would lead everyone in a time of worship. I still can remember the volume of their voices as we sang, "*I stand, I stand in awe of you. I stand I stand in awe of you. Holy God to whom all praise is due, I stand in awe of you.*"

On our last night, we stayed at a hotel on the beach. Moved by the events of the past week, I asked dad if I could spend some time with God by the water. Mom would have never let me, but dad said, "Fine." Sitting on the sand, strumming and singing over the ocean I heard words in Spanish behind me. Startled, I looked into the darkness and saw two sets of eyes shining in the moonlight. Two little boys in tattered shorts and dirty, bare feet walked out of shadows. They were from the neighboring country of The Dominican Republic. They stood smiling, and pointed at my shoes, my new preacher sneakers. I had the newest pair of Nike tennis shoes you could get. As we struggled to communicate, they kept pointing and smiling. That night, I gave my preacher sneakers away. In that moment God filled my heart with a rush of joy. Over the years God has more than provided. Today, I've got a closet full of shoes. We have six kids, and all have a closet full as well.

Second Corinthians 9:6-7 says, "Remember this: Whoever sows sparingly will also reap sparingly, and whoever sows generously will also reap generously. Each of you should give what you have decided in your heart to give, not reluctantly or under compulsion, for God loves a cheerful giver." Notice the last phrase. Here's what God loves. God loves a cheerful giver.

Jesus said in John 6:35, "I am the bread of life; whoever comes to me shall not hunger, and whoever believes in me shall never thirst."

When we put our faith in Jesus, the bread of life, he satisfies the only need we really have, the need for him.

So, let's put away grumbling and choose praise. First Thessalonians 5:18 says, "Give thanks in all circumstances; for this is the will of God in Christ Jesus for you." Some say, "I'll thank him after my breakthrough." The Bible doesn't say thank him after, but thank him in every circumstance.

If you don't thank him now you won't when you arrive. If you can't worship in the wilderness there will be only worry when you reach the Promised Land. If there's no gratitude now you'll be a grouch on the other side. If you can't praise him today you'll be proud tomorrow.

You don't learn gratitude in the Promised Land. You learn thankfulness on the backside of the desert. Thank him in every circumstance. Right now is the right time, the only time. Be present where you are. You only have now, not later.

You'll never know he is the answer until you praise him through your problems. Lift up your voice. While you're walking through, Jesus is working it out. Praise him in your marriage now. Praise him in your career. Praise him in your family situation. Praise him in the house you're living in right now. Right now is the right time to praise the Lord.

Your old outlook on life will get an extreme makeover. The atmosphere in your home will go from heavy to happy. Your mourning and sorrow will turn to joy. Turn your pouting to praise and the devil will flee from you! If you thank him in every circumstance, God will provide for your needs and bring you through the "in betweens" to his Promised Land.

10

Leadershift

"But we will give ourselves continually to prayer,
and to the ministry of the word." (Acts 6:4)

W hen I was about 16 years old, the worship pastor at dad's
church resigned unexpectedly. With nowhere else to turn, dad
asked if I would fill in. I had been taking piano lessons and knew how
to chord a bit. But all the songs I knew were in the key of G, and my
voice sounded like Bob Dylan. To my surprise, we made it through
the first Sunday and the Sunday after that. A short-term assignment
turned into a few years.

My younger brother Charlie was learning to play the bass guitar,
so he got recruited also. We had an old brown and white Rickenbacker
with strings that had not been changed in ten years. Back on the black
Tama drums was our older and wiser youth pastor.

Slowly our repertoire of tunes grew. The hot worship songs of this
bygone era were piano-driven, with a key change to build momentum.
We started moving in this direction. Charlie did his best but always
managed to hit several bonkers.

After a long rehearsal, my patience would wear thin. He sat behind
me on stage. If he missed a note, I would turn around, glare and cross
my eyebrows. He grew tired of this quickly. One Sunday, after a big

bunch of fret buzz and bonkers, I turned to give him the dagger eyes of correction. I was surprised to see him smiling back this time. More dagger eyes only caused him to chuckle harder. Our youth pastor was also laughing. I finished and walked away, wondering what was so funny.

I had no idea my brother had wiped a big booger on the back of my suit coat. That's right. We did church in suits, ties, and starched shirts in those days. I played on stage with his dried snot hanging off, and I never knew. Revenge is sweet. But the real booger on my back was my pride, and lack of patience.

All of us have blind spots, areas of weakness we can't see. They are like giant boogers on our backs. As gifted as Moses was, he had a giant booger. He could write holy Scripture, spend hours in prayer, part seas, and call down plagues, but was horrible at organization. As we read Exodus 18, it's almost humorous to see how clueless poor Moses was. He saw the big picture but didn't understand how to administrate and make it flow.

The church Moses led was over a million strong. Because there were no systems and structures in place, the burden fell on his shoulders. Not knowing what to do, humble Moses hunkered down to carry the weight alone. As a result, the great congregation in the wilderness struggled along at a snail's pace and began to grow tired and discouraged.

The breakthrough Moses needed came through a relationship. When God wants to raise us to a new level, this is his preferred method. Relationships are the key to life. The answer to the thorny issue hidden in the mysterious mist of our frustration often comes through friendship.

Truth #10–To last in leadership, you must do less and delegate more.

Exodus 18:1 says, "Now Jethro, the priest of Midian and father-in-law of Moses, heard of everything God had done for Moses and for his people Israel, and how the Lord had brought Israel out of Egypt."

Growing up in Pharaoh's palace, Moses never really knew his dad. When he was 40 and a fugitive, he ran into Jethro. This priest of Median and follower of Yahweh took him in, gave him a job and his daughter Zipporah. Hundreds of miles from his people, Moses found a spiritual father figure. While Jethro was a gift, Moses was a blessing as well. After living with seven daughters all his life, Jethro finally had a son. But after the burning bush and 40 years of service, Moses took his family and headed back to Egypt.

Finally, Jethro received an update. Most likely, the news came through Zipporah. Moses had sent her back (Exodus 18:2) possibly for her own protection. She came back to dad and shared the amazing news. Moses, the misfit prince, had overcome mighty Pharaoh and freed the Israelites from slavery. The refugee of Egypt, the stuttering shepherd, was now leading the people of God to the land of promise. Jethro was blown away.

Zipporah arrived with their two sons, Gershom and Eliezer. We find their names in Exodus 18:3. Gershom, whose name means "a foreigner there," was born while Moses was on the run in Midian. The name of the second son was Eliezer, which means "my God is my helper." Parents think long and hard about the names of their children. We don't want to be like the boxer George Foreman, who gave his seven sons the same name—George Edward Foreman. On his website, Foreman says he did this so his sons would always have something in common. We want to know what a name means. The births of our children mark the most important seasons in our lives. For Moses, the names of his sons told the story. In his early years, he felt like a foreigner with no place to call home. But the God he came to know and love was his helper and deliverer.

Exodus 18:5 says, "Jethro, Moses' father-in-law, together with Moses' sons and wife, came to him in the wilderness, where he was camped near the mountain of God." Jethro heard the Israelites were camping near his home, at the mountain of God. He packed the RV and headed into the wilderness to reunite the family. As they drew closer, he sent word ahead, "Get ready! I've got the wife and the kids in tow!"

Think of the joy a soldier in Afghanistan would experience if his family showed up by surprise. Moses couldn't wait and went out to meet them. Lots of hugs and kisses for everyone. There was so much to share. Jethro was overjoyed. He lifted his voice and exclaimed in Exodus 18:10, "Praise be to the Lord!"

I'm a Moses fan. I want to read how he grabbed his wife and kids and got away to reconnect. But notice Exodus 18:13, "The next day Moses took his seat to serve as judge for the people, and they stood around him from morning till evening." The very next day, caught up in the rush, like a twig in the rapids, he sped past his family with a cup of joe in his hand. He worked from morning until evening, as the people stood around waiting in the hot sun.

Second to Chinese water torture is having to stand in a long, slow-moving line. Notice again Exodus 18:13, "The next day Moses took his seat to serve as judge for the people, and they stood around him from morning till evening." These good people evidently had some significant issues causing tremendous pain.

The other day we pulled up to Chick-fil-A. Because it was lunchtime, the cars were bumper to bumper, wrapped around the restaurant. We decided to use a stopwatch and see how long it would take. We had our food in six minutes. Smiling faces with iPads took our order outside, asking, "How can I serve you?" They had two lines moving, and team members working like bees in a hive. I wanted to get back in line it was so fun. But Moses was all alone, trying to serve everyone's needs.

Jethro watched as the line inched along. Exodus 18:14 says, "... his father-in-law saw all that Moses was doing for the people..." No murmuring from Moses. He was willing to sacrifice everything for the call. He had a sincere desire to be obedient and faithful – to hear God say, "Well done."

Watching from a distance, Jethro could see this was not a sustainable ministry model. Finally, he asked in Exodus 8:13, "What is this you are doing for the people? Why do you alone sit as judge, while all these people stand around you from morning till evening?"

Moses responded in Exodus 18:15, "Because the people come to me to seek God's will." If you agree to do it all, the people will show up and stand around and watch as you wear yourself out. But even the Son of God had physical limitations, and could not heal every sickness and save every soul.

Ministry can become a hidden addiction and secret obsession. We love feeling needed like an addict loves crack. It's called "helper's high." So hooked on fixing problems we can't see our life becoming a problem.

It's a rush to play the role of personal Jesus for our community. But our job is not to crucify ourselves to save others. We're to connect them to the Savior, the one who will never leave or forsake them, their ever-present help in time of need. The joy of sacrifice in time turns to pain when we run out of steam. That pain turns to bitterness, and we become angry at the people we once loved.

While we try and nurse the smoldering wick back to life, the people we gave it all for will pack up and leave for the next big thing. In just a short while, as Moses spent time alone with God on the mountain to refresh his soul, this same group came to Aaron and said in Exodus 32:1, "Come, make us gods who will go before us. As for this fellow Moses who brought us up out of Egypt, we don't know what has happened to him."

Notice Jethro's indirect approach. "Hey, just curious. Why are you doing everything?" Moses answered, "Can't you see? These people need me." In the shortest verse of the chapter, Jethro said in Exodus 18:17, "What you are doing is not good." When I was a young kid I had nasty case of athletes' foot. I had oozing blisters all over my feet and in between my toes and had no idea what to do. My grandma Whitlow saw me limping, and took off my shoes and smelly socks. She said,

"What you're doing is not good." She proceeded to pop those blisters and rub in Absorbine Junior. I thought she lit my feet on fire. As I writhed in pain, she smiled and said it would be all right.

We can limp through life, irritated and frustrated without knowing why. The more we scratch the mysterious fungus from hell, the worse it gets. A wise friend, mentor, or counselor can observe and ask the right questions. As they pull back the layers and start popping blisters, it will sting. When their questions make you squirm, you've found the source of the problem. That's where healing begins.

Moses was no spring chicken. He was in the final third of his life at 80 years of age. He still had much to do, like write the Torah, build the Tabernacle, and lead the people to Canaan. But he was sitting alone, settling disputes all day like a parent correcting rowdy kids in the back of a station wagon. Moses was working in what has been called the "drudgery zone," those activities that drain our energy and yield meager results.

Let's pause for a moment. The work God has for you is too great to do alone. God was already preparing Moses for this realization. Just before Jethro's visit, the Amalekites attacked Israel from behind. Moses went up on a nearby mountain while Joshua fought below. As long as Moses held up his hands the Israelites prevailed, but whenever he lowered them, the Amalekites got the upper hand. As the day wore on, the Bible says in Exodus 17:12, "Moses' hands grew tired…" The Hebrew word for "grew tired" is *kabad*, and it means heavy, grievous, severe, and sorrowful. It is the same word used in Exodus 18:18 when Jethro said, "the work is too heavy (*kabad*) for you." This is how we feel when most of our precious time is spent in the drudgery zone, heavy and tired. But as his hands began to tremble and fall, Aaron and Hur were there to help. They slid a stone over for him to sit on, and held his hands up until the battle was won.

Jethro said to Moses, "If you try to do it alone, you will wear yourself out." Have you ever felt worn out? If you try and do it alone, you'll either burn out or hang on until the bitter end like a shriveled leaf on a barren tree in the middle of winter. You'll end up droopy, saggy, and sad. No one wants to follow a droopy, sad leader no matter how devoted and devout they are.

Here's the danger. The "helper's high" you once craved will no longer stimulate or soothe. Like a drug addict grows tired of dope, you'll start looking for a higher high. Instead of reaching out for help, you might hide in shame, feeling like a failure. Alone, tempted, and discouraged, a leader can then fall into a snare of temptation. Usually it's a moment's release, a fleeting pleasure, a silly fling. Like Esau, who gave up his birthright for a bowl of soup, they throw it all away. In the end, everything they worked and sacrificed for comes tumbling down like a house of cards.

To finish the race marked out for you, don't wear yourself out. Take time to fill the tank. As we lead others, we must rediscover and invest in those activities that bring joy and renewal. So, ask yourself this important question, "What do I enjoy doing?" Then put it on the calendar and do it.

Having put his finger on the issue, Moses was all ears. Jethro proceeded to clarify the tasks needing Moses' full attention. It wasn't a complicated job description. Let's keep it simple. We don't need 40 tasks on our to do list. Just three areas to focus on. Let's look at each closely so we might learn how to lead through our wilderness journey to the Promised Land. He said in Exodus 18:19, "Listen now to me and I will give you some advice, and may God be with you. You must be the people's representative before God and bring their disputes to him."

First, you must have a strong prayer life. Moses' number one job was to pray and intercede for the people. If we're always putting out fires, we can overlook our most important ministry. To find the energy for the work ahead, even Jesus got up early to spend time with his Father. Mark 1:35 says, "Very early in the morning, while it was still dark, Jesus got up, left the house and went off to a solitary place, where he prayed."

When shouldering the burdens of the people, we must cast our cares on the one who cares for us. Let's never forget, the greatest appointment on the calendar each day is with God in prayer. Hudson Taylor, the founder of the China Inland Mission, once wrote, "Do not have your concert first and then tune your instrument afterwards. Begin the day with the Word of God and prayer, and get first of all into harmony with Him."

Second, you must be faithful to teach. Jethro continued in Exodus 18:20, "Teach them his decrees and instructions, and show them the way they are to live and how they are to behave." In the Hebrew, the word for "teach" is *zahar* and it also means shine, or be a light. Instead of leading each person through the dark, Moses needed to shine the light—God's principles for living.

Remember, the apostles of the early church felt the tug to divert their attention from prayer and study of Scripture. But they said in Act 6:4, "...we will give our attention to prayer and the ministry of the word." Paul exhorted a young pastor named Timothy to, "Study to show thyself approved unto God, a workman that needeth not to be ashamed, rightly dividing the word of truth." (2 Timothy 2:15, KJV). Study time is work time. Our tools are not hammers, saws, and measuring tapes, but the Word of God, and any study aids that might bring additional insight. Before we are teachers, we must first be students. Labor well, so you can divide, organize, and present the word of truth. If you will feed, the flock will follow your lead.

Moses had the natural bent for the first two assignments. But there was one other essential responsibility for the congregation to flourish. Jethro continued in Exodus 18:21, "But select capable men from all the people—men who fear God, trustworthy men who hate dishonest gain—and appoint them as officials over thousands, hundreds, fifties and tens."

To thrive in the wilderness, he had to delegate and empower others. Instead of doing everything while everyone watched, he had to start leading. He needed to build a team with each person serving in their giftedness and capacity. Moses couldn't shoulder the burden alone, but a team pulling in the same direction could meet every need.

How do we build a team? According to Exodus 18:21 we need to first select capable people. This is not an advertisement on the website for anyone interested. We must be selective. One quality of a capable person is their ability to solve problems. We want positive people who bring solutions to the meeting.

Also, they must fear God, or have a sense of awe, respect, and reverence for the Lord. This is more important than charisma, the ability to woo, or the gift of gab. They don't need to be perfect angels. But they should be eager to take the next step in their relationship with Jesus.

They should also be trustworthy and dependable. When the time comes to purchase a new car, we all want reliability. The bells and whistles are nice, but will it start at 5 AM when it's below zero and we need to get to work? Don't make an impulse buy when the latest hotrod rolls in. Before you give a title out, allow someone to prove themselves in a smaller way. Before setting them over thousands, ask them if they would be OK leading a small group of five.

Finally, Jethro advised Moses to appoint them. This requires an uncomfortable degree of risk, like putting in a freshman quarterback in the final seconds of the fourth quarter with the championship on the line. But, you can't wear the headset, coach the team, and play quarterback at the same time.

Notice Proverbs 14:4 from the NLT, "Without oxen a stable stays clean, but you need a strong ox for a large harvest." The only good thing about a one-man show is that everything stays neat. On the downside, you have no harvest and starve to death. It's risky and sometimes smelly, but the reward is worth it. A culture of delegation and empowerment will attract other leaders. If you hold the ministry too tightly, you'll squeeze the life out of it.

In the painting *Flight of Fancy* by Magaritte, we see a painter putting the finishing touches on a bird taking flight, with majestic outstretched wings. The artist's head is turned to the left and focused intently on an egg sitting on a table. Instead of seeing an old egg, he envisioned what the egg would become. May God give us the vision to see the potential in others instead of magnifying their faults.

Nick Sabin, the football coach for the Alabama Tide, has won eight national championships, nine SEC titles and is still going strong at 69. At just 15 years old, his coach at Monongah High School in West Virginia saw something special in him. As a young sophomore, he made him the starting quarterback of the varsity team and allowed him to call the plays from the huddle. Their team went on to win the state title. The way we see others can cause them to soar to greater heights.

Jethro wrapped it up with this promise in Exodus 18:23, "If you do this and God so commands, you will be able to stand the strain, and all these people will go home satisfied." I can see Jethro pointing at the Disney-like line as he said, "If you do this, all these people will go home satisfied." The Hebrew word for "satisfied" is *shalom*, and is most often translated peace. It is a rich, multifaceted word that means wholeness, contentment, prosperity, and tranquility.

How would 80 year-old Moses respond? Though advanced in years, he was not set in his ways. He was a humble, life-long learner. Exodus 18:24 says, "Moses listened to his father-in-law and did everything he said."

11

Don't Waste Your Wilderness

These things happened to them as examples and
were written down as warnings for us, on whom the
culmination of the ages has come. (1 Corinthians 10:11)

The word "wilderness" occurs over 300 times in the Bible. It was hot,
barren, and brown – far away from the hubbub of daily life. It was
a place of danger, wild animals, and exposure to the natural elements.

Whenever God wanted to do something special in someone's life,
he first led them into the wilderness. Moses received his call, David
wrote his greatest songs, Elijah heard the still small voice of God,
John the Baptist prepared the way for the Lord, and Jesus received
fresh power from the Holy Spirit after 40 days in the wilderness.
Surrounded by nothing they discovered God was everything they
needed. The wasteland became a place of abundance, beauty, and personal transformation.

After three months of following the cloud, the Israelites came to
the foot of Mount Sinai and began setting up camp. As the last tent
stakes were driven into the ground, the Lord came down on top of
the mountain. It began to shake and billow smoke like a giant furnace.
Lightning shot through the plumes and thunder cracked overhead

like breaking trees. A loud trumpet blasted as pillars of fire struck the summit. There was no denying it. Here was the mountain-moving God.

This was a special moment, like a wedding in the desert. God was about to establish a special covenant relationship with Israel. He called Moses up to go over the guidelines. It started with the Ten Commandments, simple rules to help the Israelites live a better life – good things like love God, don't lie, don't steal, don't kill, love your spouse, and honor dad and mom. God also laid out plans for a place of worship, a tent in the wilderness, where he would live in the middle of their camp.

But Exodus 32:1 says, "When the people saw that Moses was so long in coming down from the mountain, they gathered around Aaron and said, 'Come, make us gods who will go before us. As for this fellow Moses who brought us up out of Egypt, we don't know what has happened to him.'"

Moses was taking too long. Irritated and impatient they gathered around Aaron and said, "We're tired of sitting around. Make us a god to lead us out of here."

We all want Aaron to be strong, and to challenge the people to hold on. But, without a brother to lean on, Aaron was weak as water. God had blessed him with many gifts. He was a good communicator, but also a talented artist. He called everyone to bring their gold earrings. He melted the precious metal, and used his God-given abilities to fashion a golden calf.

Back in Egypt a number of their gods were portrayed as cows, a symbol of strength and power. The people liked his work. They said, "Everyone, these are the gods who brought us out of Egypt!" (Exodus 32:4)

When Aaron saw their approval, he went a step further. Exodus 32:5 says, "When Aaron saw this, he built an altar in front of the calf and announced, 'Tomorrow there will be a festival to the Lord.'"

There was no sleeping in the next day. The people rose up early and brought their best offerings to the golden cow. After worship, they began to party. The more they drank, the more their little get-together became a flaming rave. Soon, right there by the mountain of God, they were letting it all hang out.

God saw it and became angry. He told Moses he wanted to destroy the Israelites and start over with him. But Moses interceded, stood in the gap, and pleaded for grace. Exodus 32:14 says, "Then the Lord relented and did not bring on his people the disaster he had threatened." The God who toppled Pharaoh, parted the sea, and shook Sinai, allowed himself to be moved by the prayers of one man. Israel was saved yet again.

Moses came down from the mountain and what did he see? Exodus 32:25 says, "Moses saw that the people were running wild and that Aaron had let them get out of control and so become a laughingstock to their enemies." This is a nice way of saying they were running around naked and engaging in sexual sin. Looking back on this event, the Apostle Paul wrote in 1 Corinthians 10:7-8, "Do not be idolaters, as some of them were; as it is written: 'The people sat down to eat and drink and got up to indulge in revelry.' We should not commit sexual immorality, as some of them did—and in one day twenty-three thousand of them died." So, the people of God became a laughingstock to their enemies.

It was like a parent coming home early from a long trip to find their teen throwing a raging house party. Pictures hanging crooked from the pulsating music. House trashed. Strangers in each room. Moses raised the stone tablets engraved with the Ten Commandments and shattered them on the ground. By the mountain, Israel broke the covenant of blessing God hoped to make.

Wanting them to remember the bitterness of their offense, Moses made a special kind of smoothie. He ground their golden calf into powder, mixed it with water and made them drink it. How foolish they were to trust a man-made deity. Their god could be ground up, swallowed, and passed out of their bodies as human waste. Their holy cow wasn't worth a turd.

Moses then went over to his brother and asked the question of the hour. "How could you lead the people into such sin right here at the foot of God's mountain?" Too ashamed to take responsibility, he offered a creative but lame excuse, "They gave me their gold. When I threw it in the fire out came this calf." (Exodus 32:24). Like a Pop-Tart in a toaster, out popped the golden calf.

Some were upset at Moses for destroying their cow. It was time to take a stand. He raised his voice and asked the ultimate question in Exodus 32:26, "Who is on the Lord's side?" It was a moment of decision. For those still defiant and divisive, Moses sent out the Levites with swords. They killed 3,000 rebels, and God struck many others with a plague. How sad. The wedding in the wilderness turned into a train wreck.

Truth #11–In the wilderness of waiting, God is working.

Exodus 32:1 again says, "When the people saw that Moses was so long in coming down from the mountain…" Has it ever felt like God was taking so long? In the COVID-19 pandemic we all got sick of waiting for the vaccine, for schools to start, for life to get back to normal. We grew tired of watching cornhole competitions on ESPN. It was tough doing church online as kids threw Cheerios at the TV.

Though it seems like everything is taking forever, God is moving in the earth today. Again, with the golden calf catastrophe in mind, Paul wrote in 1 Corinthians 10:11, "These things happened to them as examples and were written down as warnings for us, on whom the culmination of the ages has come."

Think about a fireworks show on the fourth of July. You have your family on a grassy spot, lying down, ready to take it all in. There's patriotic music, mixed with a steady boom of canon fire, followed by explosions of light in the night sky. Honestly, after about 20 minutes, we all get a little bored. But at the highest moment, the final two minutes, all the canons shoot continuous rounds in quick succession. The music builds. You sit up, point your finger and try not to blink. Your family has waited patiently to see the end of the show. The final two minutes are always the best part.

We're living in the final two minutes, what the Bible calls the culmination of the ages. The great Author of Life is bringing history, His story, into the final chapter, and the climactic end. We don't know when but we're closer to the return of Jesus than ever. 1 Thessalonians 5:2 says, "For you know quite well that the day of the Lord's return will come unexpectedly, like a thief in the night."

To help us stay on track God inspired Moses long ago to write these things down for our benefit. We're living in an even greater time. The Old Covenant has passed and in Jesus the New Covenant of grace has come. By faith the laws of God are written on our hearts. Every believer can be empowered by the Holy Spirit for ministry and witness.

Though we might not see it, this is our moment by the mountain. God is working even now. For example, in Iran about 500 Muslims come to faith in Christ every month. And most of the new believers are young as 70 percent of Iran's populations is under 30. Until 1960 Christians were forbidden to live in Nepal. But today, in all 75 districts, there is a church with believers numbering about half a million (Operation World). In China about 10,000 to 25,000 come to faith in Christ every day, bringing the Christian population to about 60 to 80 million (Open Doors). In the first century there were 360 unbelievers for every one believer. But today there are fewer than seven for every Christian (Vision 2020–https://www.prayerfoundation.org/world christian_growth_statistics.htm). We are seeing Habakkuk 2:14 come to pass in our day, "For the earth will be filled with the knowledge of the glory of the LORD as the waters cover the sea."

So how do we keep our hearts and minds focused and alert while we wait by the mountain for Jesus to return? First, to survive and thrive we need Christian connection and fellowship. It's hard to imagine Aaron making an idol, then proclaiming, "Tomorrow we'll hold a festival to the Lord." Moses' older brother and spokesmen gave the sacred name of Yahweh to his golden cow. All alone, Aaron was quickly cowed by the crowd. Even the strongest become weak when everyone around is pulling them down. First Corinthians 10:12 says, "So, if you think you are standing firm, be careful that you don't fall!"

The giant sequoia trees in northern California are a national treasure and natural wonder. They can grow over 200 feet tall, and live for thousands of years. The General Sherman is the largest tree on earth measuring 275 feet tall, 25 foot in diameter, and is over 2500 years old. You would think a tree that tall would have deep roots. But in fact, their roots only go about six to seven feet below the earth. Instead of going down, they spread out and interlock with other redwood trees, like a team of rugby players locking arms. Connected together they stand stronger. It's good to have neighbors who will lend you an egg, some flour, or watch the kids in a pinch. But let's make a commitment to get deeply rooted in a local church, with a family of believers in Christian community.

Second, we must watch out for the spiral of ingratitude. No one wakes up one day and says, "Let's get crazy, and let it all hang out." It's a slow spiral downward. We see it spelled out in Romans 1:21-25. It seems like the Apostle Paul had Exodus 32 in mind.

> For although they knew God, they neither glorified him as God nor gave thanks to him, but their thinking became futile and their foolish hearts were darkened. Although they claimed to be wise, they became fools and exchanged the glory of the immortal God for images made to look like a mortal human being and

birds and animals and reptiles. Therefore God gave them over in the sinful desires of their hearts to sexual impurity for the degrading of their bodies with one another. They exchanged the truth about God for a lie, and worshiped and served created things rather than the Creator—who is forever praised. Amen.

The downward spiral starts by refusing to acknowledge God and express thanks, much like an ungrateful child snubbing mom on Mother's Day. The heart and mind become dark and confused. Next, you give your devotion and affection to created things instead of the Creator. After being rejected continually, God lifts his restraining hand of grace. In the end, you're left like helpless prey to the hungry wolves of your sinful passions.

Romans 1:24 says, "...for the degrading of their bodies with one another." When you degrade something, you don't use it properly, in the way it was designed. Recently, my son and I went to Walmart for new fishing gear. We bought a couple open-face reels and headed for the intracoastal waterway. About an hour into our excursion, he grew tired of waiting for a fish. That's when I heard a strange garbling noise. When I looked over, he had his brand new reel under the salt water, cranking away—garble, garble, garble. I said, "What are you doing?" He said, "I like the noise. It's so cool!" I said, "Son, you can't crank your rod like that in the saltwater. Stay focused. It's time to catch some fish." But sure enough, a few minutes later, I heard the same garble garble noise. The next day his new reel was rusted, jammed, and ruined.

Though written 2,000 years ago, Romans 1 describes where the spiral of ingratitude leads. Paul would go on to write in verses 26-27:

For this reason God gave them up to dishonorable passions. For their women exchanged natural relations for those that are contrary to nature; and the men likewise gave up natural relations with women and were consumed with passion for one another, men committing shameless acts with men and receiving in themselves the due penalty for their error.

We're moving ancient boundaries, and redefining laws established by our Creator. Claiming to be wise, we've made things really confusing. While we wait, let's choose to be thankful and honor God with our bodies, the temple of the Holy Spirit.

Remember Moses' question to the Israelites, "Who is on the Lord's side?" What's your answer? A generation later, Joshua asked the same question to wavering Israelites, still wrestling with the idols their parents worshipped in Egypt. In Joshua 24:15 he said, "Choose you this day who you will serve…as for me and my house we will serve the Lord."

See your season of waiting in the wilderness as an opportunity. It is a season of preparation and blessing. While you wait, God is working in the world. Every day we're moving closer and closer to the glorious day of the Lord's return. This is our moment by the mountain. Decide today to be on the Lord's side. Choose to be rooted with his people in fellowship. Let's keep our eyes on the Promised Land. The Message version of 1 Peter 4:3; 7 says, "You've already put in your time in that God-ignorant way of life, partying night after night, a drunken and profligate life. Now it's time to be done with it for good… Everything in the world is about to be wrapped up, so take nothing for granted. Stay wide-awake in prayer."

12

Experiencing the Presence of God

> You make known to me the path of life; you will
> fill me with joy in your presence, with eternal
> pleasures at your right hand. (Psalm 16:11)

The massive Lincoln Memorial in Washington, DC portrays our greatest president as polished, and properly groomed. However, history tells a different story. President Abraham Lincoln was oblivious to fashion and the styling of his hair. His lack of polish often made others point and snicker.

For example, Lincoln once visited New England to see his son Robert at school. Robert and his friends were invited to hear him speak and about 500 people turned out. The politicians in New England took great pride in their dress. But when Lincoln showed up, Robert's friends were shocked. He was tall and awkward, sporting black, baggy, high-water trousers. His hair was uncombed, his neck tie cranked to one side. His legs were so long they couldn't fit under the table.

One of the boys remarked, "Isn't it a shame that Robert's dad is so homely? Don't you feel sorry for him?" In David Herbert Donald's biography of Lincoln, he writes, "But after Lincoln disentangled his legs, rose slowly from his chair, and began speaking, they forgot his appearance; they no longer pitied Robert but felt proud to know his father."

In our age we too are fixated on appearance. Image is everything. Selfies are carefully chosen and digitally enhanced. To cut a fashionable figure, some squeeze into a pair of Spanx. Even the name sounds painful. The restrictive garment squeezes the flab and holds it all in place. The only problem is you can't breathe.

There will always be someone more beautiful, muscular, and better dressed. In an increasingly post-Christian world, what distinguishes us as God's people? Like Lincoln, it's what's on the inside. It's the presence of God in our lives. Notice Moses' prayer in Exodus 33:15-16, "If your Presence does not go with us, do not send us up from here. How will anyone know that you are pleased with me and with your people unless you go with us? What else will distinguish me and your people from all the other people on the face of the earth?"

The "presence of God" makes us think of the sweet by and by. Some see streets of gold, smiling angels strumming harps, while robed choirs sing in the clouds. But the presence of God is something we can experience here and now.

In fact, it's the reason you were created. I'm not sure what you do for a living, but your career is not your ultimate calling. More than making a buck or a bonus, God created you to live in relationship with him and to enjoy his presence.

In the Hebrew language the word for "presence" is *panim*, and it literally means "face." We experience someone's presence when they turn their face toward us. Notice this prayer in Psalm 4:6, "Many, LORD, are asking, 'Who will bring us prosperity?' Let the light of your face shine on us."

God is more than a general presence, running the universe, making stars and sunshine. God wants to show up in a personal way to bless, encourage, and strengthen you. Nothing on the planet compares to the light of his face—no drug, excursion, or encounter. No outfit, purse, or hairdo could ever come close to the presence of God. Psalm 16:11 says, "You make known to me the path of life; you will fill me with joy in your presence, with eternal pleasures at your right hand." Psalm 103:5 tells us God's presence "…satisfies your desires with good things so that your youth is renewed like the eagle's."

Truth #12–God's presence is your lifeline.

All through the book of Exodus we see the presence of God—at the burning bush, parting the Red Sea, the pillar of fire, the cloud leading the children of God through the wilderness, and finally at Mt. Sinai. But as we saw in the last chapter, that's when the Israelites grew tired of waiting and made a golden cow. They called their creation "the Lord," and worshipped it. Things quickly turned into a mess. Exodus 33:1-3 tells us what happened next, "Then the Lord said to Moses, 'Leave this place, you and the people you brought up out of Egypt, and go up to the land I promised on oath to Abraham, Isaac and Jacob… But I will not go with you, because you are a stiff-necked people…'"

God gave Moses devastating news—"I will not go with you." Notice he said, "You take your people you brought out of Egypt." Have you ever said that to your spouse after the kids embarrassed you at the grocery store? "Can you take these kids of yours and go somewhere?"

God no longer wanted to associate with the Israelites because they were "stiff-necked." Every Israelite understood the metaphor. In an agrarian culture, a busy farmer had no time for a stubborn ox. With work to be done, they dug in their hoofs, stiffened their necks, and turned their heads to stare back at the frustrated farmer with one defiant eye. God's people were as ornery as a wild ox. So he said, "I'm done. Time to separate. You guys go to the Promised Land. I'm not going."

I'm a southern boy. If someone doesn't want to accept an invitation they'll often say, "Ya'll go on ahead." God was saying, "Ya'll go on ahead. I will not bless this with my presence."

If our hearts are stubborn and hard, we can end up doing life without the presence of God. It's possible to do church without God's presence. It's called the frozen chosen. We can do marriage and family without God's presence. We can journey through the wilderness of life, trying to reach our Promised Land without the joy of his presence. So, how do we experience God's presence?

First, we humble ourselves. Exodus 33:4 says, "When the people heard these distressing words, they began to mourn and no one put on any ornaments." As they walked out of captivity, the Egyptians gave them gold and silver jewelry. By Mount Sinai they were dressed to impress. The sunlight glistened off the gold chains around their necks. But convicted of sin, they took off their ornaments as a sign of inward humility.

If there's one thing that repels my wife, its gas—belching, burping, flagellating. It's a big turn off. Nothing makes her run to the other side of the house faster. The one thing that repels the presence of God is the gas of pride. He won't come near it. He won't bless a proud heart with his presence. Psalm 138:6 says, "For though the LORD is high, he regards the lowly, but the haughty he knows from afar." And James 4:6 says, "…God opposes the proud but shows favor to the humble."

Second, we must trust in Jesus for grace. Moses provides an example of Jesus' ministry for us. Old Moses never stopped praying for the children of Israel. Even though they criticized and complained, he never gave up. When God wanted to wipe them out and start over, he stepped in to plead for mercy. Moses' prayers moved the heart of God. Psalm 106:23 says, "So he said he would destroy them—had not Moses, his chosen one, stood in the breach before him to keep his wrath from destroying them."

In Jesus we have the greatest intercessor of all. Hebrews 7:25 says, "Therefore he is able to save completely those who come to God through him, because he always lives to intercede for them." Moses eventually died at the ripe old age of 120. But Jesus always lives to intercede for us. In the mystery of the Trinity that is God—Father, Son, and Holy Spirit—Jesus is the one covering our shortcomings with grace. Like a mother never stops praying for her children, Jesus never gives up on us.

I think of our daughter Sierra, the one who stands in the breach for Mowgli, our dog. Whenever he makes a mess, she's quick to cover it up. If anyone tries to torment her precious pet, she's there to intercede. With Sierra as his advocate Mowgli will be safe forever. First John 2:1 says, "My dear children, I write this to you so that you will not sin. But if anybody does sin, we have an advocate with the Father—Jesus Christ, the Righteous One."

Third, we make space to spend time with God. Where did Moses go to pray in the middle of the wilderness, surrounded by a million grouchy Israelites? Exodus 33:7 says, "Now Moses used to take a tent and pitch it outside the camp some distance away, calling it the tent of meeting." As people set up their RV's, picnic tables, tents, chairs, and gathered firewood, Moses went some distance away to pitch "the tent of meeting."

Exodus 33:11 says, "The Lord would speak to Moses face to face, as one speaks to a friend…" The presence of God was always around in a general sense. But when Moses showed up at the tent, they spent time connecting like old friends.

I think about our home. My amazing wife Wendy runs our house, managing the details of our six children. Her desk is by the refrigerator, the center of activity. I know she's there in a general sense. We text and email. But to grow our relationship we have to turn our faces to one another, giving our undivided attention. In that moment we experience one another's presence.

What's your camp like? The cell phone buzzes and beckons. You just got four new likes on Instagram. The dead 9 volt batteries in the fire alarms are chirping like a flock of birds. The kids are fighting. The toilet is overflowing. The dog just barfed on the couch. Where's your "tent of meeting"? The God of the universe wants to show up and spend time with you as a friend.

Speaking of place, Susanna Wesley, the mother of evangelist John and hymn writer Charles Wesley, had 19 children. She managed the house and homeschooled the kids. But she made a place. She would sit down and pull her apron over her head to spend an hour in God's word and prayer. She made it clear to the kids that while she was under the apron she was not to be interrupted. Psalm 91:1 (NKJV) says, "He who dwells in the secret place of the Most High Shall abide under the shadow of the Almighty."

We get a chance to eavesdrop as Moses prays in the tent of meeting. In his conversation with God we find three benefits that come from dwelling in God's presence. In Exodus 33:12 Moses says, "You have been telling me, 'Lead these people,' but you have not let me know whom you will send with me...'"

Moses carried a heavy burden—the realization he had to lead the people alone in the wilderness. A burden is something you'd like to change but can't. You would like it to leave but it won't. I remember one time we let a Kirby vacuum cleaner salesman into our house. After his demonstration he became a burden. We couldn't get him out the door. I almost called the cops. Burdens are like rocks we can't move. Eventually, burdens block out the presence of God.

He continues in Exodus 33:13–"...Remember that this nation is your people." Instead of sitting in the darkness of despair, we can turn each burden into prayer. "This company is your company. This family is your family. My finances are your finances. My life is your life. My future is your future. This problem is your problem. I give my burdens to you." Listen to God's response in Exodus 33:14, "My Presence will go with you, and I will give you rest."

God's presence always gives us rest. If you are tired, irritable, and overwhelmed you are carrying your own burdens, trying to do life without the presence of God. Psalm 55:22 says, "Cast your burden upon the Lord and He will sustain you; He will never allow the righteous to be shaken." Notice it doesn't tell us to share, but to throw our burdens upon the Lord. When we completely give it to the Lord he promises to sustain us.

Buoyed by the positive response, Moses pressed further in Exodus 33:15-16, "If your Presence does not go with us, do not send us up from here….What else will distinguish me and your people from all the other people on the face of the earth?"

Moses told God he would rather stay in the desert than go to the Promised Land without his presence. More than anything, Moses wanted the presence of God. The presence of God is a fragrance, an extra something, a glow, a radiance, a salty taste, a fresh breath of air that makes us stand out. People pick up on it when we walk into the room, introduce ourselves, or share an idea.

Much has been written about culture in the corporate world. Every organization wants one that's healthy and attractive. However, it's a challenge just to define the word. Many call it the intangible tangible. Culture is really the presence people sense as they interact with the organization. It could be fear, division, frustration, or negativity. On the healthier side, it could be hope, teamwork, optimism, and enthusiasm. Culture is as real as the coffee we drink. And when it's toxic it can kill an organization. Culture always trumps the message. In fact, the culture is the message.

In the corporate world we create a culture. It's our responsibility. We need to show up and communicate the kind of culture we want in words and actions. But we can't manufacture a culture of the presence of God. We can't engineer it with lights, sound, smog, great music, cool hair, and skinny jeans. We can generate a feel-good experience, but so can Disney. Without his presence our worship is just one more ditty.

Again, notice Moses interceding for wayward Israel. He didn't want the presence of God all to himself. He didn't want to make the journey to the Promised Land alone, like a monk in a monastery. So he prayed, "If your Presence does not go with us, do not send us up from here."

In this day and age some have thrown in the towel on the church. They only see the problems, irritations, and shortcomings, too numerous to count. Let's remember the church was God's idea. It's his plan to reach the world. Let's stay committed to the bride he shed his blood for. Instead of fixating on her flaws, let's intercede for God's presence to show up like never before. As Dr. Glenn Packiam writes, "The gathering is central to the church's calling and witness in the world. It is not optional or peripheral. It is the place where the people of God are formed as the family of God and filled with his Spirit so that we can be sent back into the world to reflect God's love and wisdom."

To his second request God said in Exodus 33:17, "I will do the very thing you have asked." How encouraging. God responded to Moses, "I will do the very thing you have asked."

So Moses pressed even further, praying his boldest prayer. In Exodus 33:18 he prayed, "Now show me your glory." After everything he had experienced, Moses still hungered for more of God. He wanted to see God in all his fullness.

Staring at a solar eclipse without protective glasses can cause retina damage. In the same way, the fullness of God's glory is more than our limited sensory receptors can process. But without hesitation, God still found a way to say yes. In Exodus 33:21 God said, "There is a place near me where you may stand on a rock. When my glory passes by, I will put you in a cleft in the rock and cover you with my hand until I have passed by. Then I will remove my hand and you will see my back; but my face must not be seen."

The majesty of God is described in human form, with hands, face, and back. However, because God is spirit, he's not limited to a physical body. This is a figure of speech known as an anthropomorphism—using personal traits to describe something spiritual. Here, the Bible helps our limited understanding so we can see God as personal and relational. We do not know what Moses saw when God passed by. While it was limited exposure, it was still more glory than Moses had ever seen.

After this experience he was a different person. Exodus 34:29 says, "When Moses came down from Mount Sinai...he was not aware that his face was radiant because he had spoken with the Lord." Moses was not aware that his face was radiant. After spending time in God's presence we don't have to say anything; our face is like a giant screen, displaying what our hearts and minds project. The light of God's face makes the screen of our face shine with joy. Truly we are a city set on a hill that cannot be hidden.

Moses was the only one who saw the Lord's glory on the mountain. But in Jesus the glory of God came in flesh and blood to our broken world. He didn't come to a secluded spot for a chosen few. He came for everyone to see. John 1:14 says, "The Word became flesh and made his dwelling among us. We have seen his glory, the glory of the one and only Son, who came from the Father, full of grace and truth."

The glory that Moses longed to see can be seen by anyone in the person of Jesus Christ. Hebrews 1:3 says, "And He is the radiance of His glory and the exact representation of His nature, and upholds all things by the word of His power..." What a privilege to spend personal time with Jesus. In the light of his face our lives are transformed. Nothing on earth compares to his presence. Second Corinthians 3:18 says, "And we all, who with unveiled faces contemplate the Lord's glory, are being transformed into his image with ever-increasing glory, which comes from the Lord, who is the Spirit."

Let's humble ourselves and trust in Jesus and his grace. Let's make a place and set a time. In his presence we can lay our burdens down and find rest. His presence is that extra something special, setting us apart as his people. When the light of his face shines on us, it lights up our life. May the presence of God be our most important pursuit.

13

Whose Report Will You Believe?

"What do you mean, 'If I can?'" Jesus asked. "Anything
is possible if a person believes." (Mark 9:23)

R on Howard's film *Far and Away*, starring Tom Cruise and Nicole
Kidman, begins in Ireland, where young Joe Donnelly, played by
Cruise, works for his father, a poor tenant farmer, who leases prop-
erty from a greedy landlord. Tragedy strikes when Donnelly's father
suffers a stroke and the family is evicted. Kneeling by his dying father,
young Joe hears his final words, "Land is a man's very soul. A man is
nothing without land."

With a dream in his heart, Donnelly journeys to America. Along
the way, he meets a wealthy, fiery redhead named Shannon, played by
Kidman. He does all he can to win her approval and love.

Finally, after many trials and hardships Joe mounts a horse to
claim his land in the Oklahoma Land Rush of 1889. Standing on
a 120-acre plot he triumphantly shouts, "This land is mine. Mine by
destiny!" But before he can drive in the stake to make his claim, he
fights with his chief adversary competing for Shannon's devotion. In
the melee, Donnelly's horse falls and rolls over him, crushing him

against the ground. As he lay in extreme pain, Shannon runs to his side, and he utters these words, "I know nothing of books and outfits. All I know is Joseph loves Shannon." Finally, she openly confesses her devotion to him. An injured Joe quickly revives. They grab the stake and drive it together into the ground. Chasing their dream, they end up in each other's arms, with a place to call home.

After a two year desert trek, the children of Israel finally arrive at the doorstep of Canaan. It's time to stake their claim to their land. Their season of transition is over. We can learn a lot from Israel as they stand at the threshold of a new beginning. If you're in an in-between season, here's the good news. It doesn't last forever.

In Numbers 13:1 the Lord said to Moses, "Send some men to explore the land of Canaan, which I am giving to the Israelites…" What a generous God. The former slaves of wicked Pharaoh, redeemed by God, were about to receive a huge land grant. It was not the back forty, but a land flowing with milk and honey—a place of abundance. Here the livestock could produce rich milk, and the fruit would grow as sweet as honey.

They were about to experience the fulfillment of the ancient promise given hundreds of years before to Abraham. That's why we call it the Promised Land. Genesis 15:18 says, "On that day the Lord made a covenant with Abram and said, "To your descendants I give this land…"

Imagine them working back in Goshen, making bricks of mud, and asking, "I wonder if God will keep his promise? You know the one he made to father Abraham?" And then, walking day by day in the hot sun saying, "You know I'm tired of manna soup, manna casserole, and manna burgers. Do you think God remembers that promise, you know the one he made to father Abraham?" Though it seemed liked nothing was going on, God brought his promise to pass in their day. We serve a promise-keeping God.

Exodus 13:3 continues, "So at the Lord's command Moses sent them out from the Desert of Paran. All of them were leaders of the Israelites…" Before moving into their new home, 12 scouts were sent out on a kind of Lewis and Clark expedition. Notice they were all leaders. People looked to them for guidance. The Bible is careful to list their names in Numbers 13:4-5, like a timeless memorial engraved in stone.

They explored every nook and cranny of God's great gift for 40 days. When they reached the Valley of Eshkol, they cut off a single cluster of grapes so large it took two men to carry them on a pole. Those grapes tasted amazing after eating bread for two years. I'm thinking many were relieved of constipation as well!

When they returned, the whole community gathered around, anxious to hear the news. Oddly there were two different reports. The first group spoke up. They said, "The land does flow with milk and honey. Its fruit is amazing as you can tell." Then they said the one word that changed the future of a generation – "but."

In Numbers 13:28 they continued, "But the people who live there are powerful, and the cities are fortified and very large. We even saw the descendants of Anak there." Joshua 14:15 tells us Anak was the greatest man among the Anakim, which in Hebrew means "long-necked." The opposition stood head and shoulders above the rest. Some believed they descended from the Nephilim, a powerful race of warriors living before the flood, heroes of old, men of renown.

An outbreak of murmuring spread. That's when Caleb spoke up in Numbers 13:30, "Then Caleb silenced the people before Moses and said, 'We should go up and take possession of the land, for we can certainly do it.'"

Right after Caleb spoke up, the negative spies countered in Numbers 13:31-33, "We can't attack those people; they are stronger than we are…The land we explored devours those living in it. All the people we saw there are giants…We seemed like grasshoppers in our own eyes, and we looked the same to them."

Caleb and Joshua said, "We certainly can!" The other ten said, "We certainly can't!" Their giant story kept growing. Now everyone in the land was a giant. And even more, the ground ate people for lunch. The more they talked the smaller they became. They ended up feeling like grasshoppers.

They had no idea the Canaanites had heard about their mighty God who parted the seas and defeated Pharaoh's army. Everyone knew they were coming, and were shaking in their boots (see Joshua 2:8-11). All they had to do was walk through the door and stake their claim. But instead of seeing victory they saw giants.

Truth #13–Believe the good report and you will reach the Promised Land.

The biggest giants are the ones we create in our own minds. I'm talking about limiting beliefs. Everybody is big, and "I'm so, so small." What "I can't" statements are you telling yourself? "I can't because I'm too old. I've failed too many times. I don't have enough money. I don't have enough connections. Other people are more talented and charismatic than me." The more we talk the larger our giants become.

I want to challenge you to think about your thinking. Take out a pen and a piece of paper. Get quiet. Write those "I can't" statements down and face your giants. Challenge them. Ask yourself, "Is this really true?" Watch how small your giants become.

Every giant opportunity has monster obstacles. Instead of putting our fear in giants, let's believe in our God. Ryan Holiday, in his best-selling book *The Obstacle is the Way*, encourages people to find direction by facing the challenges of life. You want to know the way? Look for an obstacle. The giant is the way. Don't run from your giants. With God fighting for us, the bigger they are, the harder they fall.

Numbers 13:32 continues, "And they spread among the Israelites a bad report about the land they had explored…" Good news takes time—a lot of social media, emails, and newsletters. It takes continual repetition for vision to gain traction. But bad news spreads like a virus. Out of the 12 spies, 10 spread a bad report about the land.

Exodus 14:1-2; 4 says, "That night all the members of the community raised their voices and wept aloud. All the Israelites grumbled against Moses and Aaron…And they said to each other, 'We should choose a leader and go back to Egypt.'" Instead of bursting with expectation, they spent the night weeping and grumbling. On the threshold of their new season, they wanted to turn around and go back to slavery in Egypt.

We must be careful who we listen to. I remember a former church member, who gave his life to Jesus, was baptized, and began attending and serving. He was a fix-it person, who always had the right tool and a willing heart. He also had a knack for conversation, making anyone feel welcome. I saw him as an up and coming leader in God's house.

But I noticed a change one day. He began talking a lot about government conspiracy theories. Come to find out, he was reading conspiracy theory magazines, blogs, and listening to podcasts. It was hopeless to fight the machine. I counseled him over and over, but he was hooked.

Then one day he injured his back. He ended up on disability and workman's comp. He couldn't leave the house. He fell into a depression. We all stopped by to say hello and to pray. Each time I saw him, it was the same old topic. The last I heard he had hired an attorney and was filing suit to get the funds for a back surgery he was convinced he needed.

Some have an evangelistic zeal to spread bad news. They are not as bright as they make themselves out to be. It takes zero talent to point at the giants. They are so large anyone can see them.

When Dabo Swinney took the coaching job for the Clemson Tigers in 2008, they were an average ACC team. Their record was seven wins and six loses. They fired Bobby Bowden in the middle of the season and made Dabo the interim coach. The giants they faced were power house recruiting machines like Alabama and Ohio State. Dabo knew their problem wasn't talent, but a lack of belief. So he came up with an idea. He made a big sign that said, "Believe" and another one that said, "I Can't" with the "t" crossed out. He carried those signs in personally to every team meeting and still does to this day. That was 2008. In 2016 and 2018 they won the National Championship, beating the Alabama Tide both times.

Realizing the importance of this moment, Joshua and Caleb did all they could to fire up the people's faith. They cried out, "The land before us is exceedingly good. We can do this because God is with us. It is already ours. We just have to stake our claim. Don't rebel against him. And don't be afraid of these people!" But it was too late. The majority of the Israelites had already chosen to believe the bad report, so Joshua and Caleb's words were like salt on their wounds. Numbers 14:10 says, "But the whole assembly talked about stoning them."

Just before they hurled the first rock, the glory of the Lord appeared. Exasperated, God asked three questions that started with the words, "how long." How long will these people treat me with contempt? How long will they refuse to believe me? How long will this wicked community grumble against me? (Numbers 14:11; 27)

Then the Lord said in Numbers 14:28, "…As surely as I live…I will do to you the very thing I heard you say." They had no idea how powerful their words were. God would do the very things they said. They said they wanted to go back, and back they would go. The land would devour them, but instead of Canaan it would be the wilderness. The spies explored the land for 40 days. This next season of wandering would take 40 years, one year for each day the spies surveyed Canaan. Everyone who grumbled and rebelled would die without receiving the promise (Numbers 14:29). The children, who they predicted would be taken as plunder, would grow up and inherit the land.

My dad had an unorthodox method for getting his kids out of bed and ready for school. He opened the door, flipped on the lights, and sang with gusto, "This is the day that the Lord has made. I will rejoice and be glad in it. Rejoice! Rejoice! I will rejoice and be glad in it. This is the day that the Lord has made." As we rubbed the boogers out, we wondered, "What is he so happy about?"

In this day and age, some would call Child Protective Services. But now that we have kids and are facing the pressures of life, I know what he was doing. He was choosing to believe a good report.

In Robert Frost's poem *The Road Not Taken*, a traveler in the wilderness of life comes to a fork in their journey.

> Two roads diverged in a yellow wood,
> And sorry I could not travel both
> And be one traveler, long I stood

At the fork, the traveler stops to consider his options. It's time to make a choice. Whose report will you believe? There's always the meeting after the meeting. The one by the water cooler, after staff. The one in the parking lot after Vision Sunday at your church.

> And looked down one as far as I could
> To where it bent in the undergrowth;
> Then took the other, as just as fair,
> And having perhaps the better claim,
> Because it was grassy and wanted wear...

He considered the popular, well-worn path, looking down to where it bent in the undergrowth. But he took the other, the grassy one, wanting wear. The highway of doubt is wide and many are they that find it.

> I shall be telling this with a sigh
> Somewhere ages and ages hence:
> Two roads diverged in a wood, and I—
> I took the one less traveled by,
> And that has made all the difference.

The brave souls who took the other path were Joshua and Caleb. And it made all the difference. When everyone packed their bags to go back to Egypt they believed the good report. Numbers 14:24 tells us why, "But because my servant Caleb has a different spirit and follows me wholeheartedly, I will bring him into the land he went to, and his descendants will inherit it."

As God promised, in time the grumblers grew weaker and died off. But Joshua and Caleb grew stronger as they waited on the Lord. When the next opportunity came 40 years later, they were ready. Listen to Caleb plead with Joshua, at 85 year of age, for the chance to take the hill country.

> So here I am today, eighty-five years old! I am still as strong today as the day Moses sent me out; I'm just as vigorous to go out to battle now as I was then. Now give me this hill country that the Lord promised me that day. You yourself heard then that the Anakites were there and their cities were large and fortified, but, the Lord helping me, I will drive them out just as he said. (Joshua 14:11-12)

Soon, God will bring you to the doorstep of a new beginning. Remember, the giant is the way. To stake your claim to the Promised Land, you must believe the good report.

Jesus said in Matthew 11:28, "Come to me, all you who are weary and burdened, and I will give you rest." Jesus is our Promised Land of rest. We don't have to fight for it. He did all the work already on the cross and in his resurrection. Believe and receive your spiritual inheritance, God's free gift of grace, forgiveness, peace, and joy. Like Caleb and Joshua, God will give you a different spirit. Ezekiel 36:26 says, "And I will give you a new heart, and I will put a new spirit in you. I will take out your stony, stubborn heart and give you a tender, responsive heart."

The Sunset Season

14

Fall at the Finish Line

> Therefore, my brothers and sisters, make every effort
> to confirm your calling and election. For if you do
> these things, you will never stumble. (2 Peter 1:10)

No study of Moses' life would be complete without looking at his fall just before the finish line. The failure in his final lap disqualified him from leading the Israelites into the Promised Land. Just before his death, on top of Mount Nebo, he saw the land from a distance. But God's last recorded words to Moses were, "...I have let you see it with your eyes, but you will not cross over into it." (Deuteronomy 34:4). If we're going to experience the good future God has planned for us, let's take a closer look at what happened and see what we can learn.

Let's be honest. Of all the books in the Bible, Numbers is probably not your favorite. Who wants to spend an afternoon at Starbucks reading lists of numerical data? But Numbers picks up where Exodus left off and tells the story of their 38-year journey from Mount Sinai to the Promised Land. In the Hebrew Bible, the book's actual title is *Bemidbar*, which means "in the desert." It's the first word of the book. Our English title comes from *Numeroi*, Jerome's title in the Latin Vulgate translation of the Bible from the fourth century AD.

In Numbers, we find God organizing the Israelites to be a blessing to the world. But there was continual unbelief, grumbling, and rebellion, in the people and the leaders, from Miriam, Aaron, and even Moses. But every time they failed, God remained faithful, keeping the ancient promise given to Abraham.

Numbers 20 contains the account of Moses' stumble. In his ministry time line, it took place during the final push to the Jordan River, in the sunset season of his leadership years. Numbers 20:1 sets the stage, "In the first month the whole Israelite community arrived at the Desert of Zin, and they stayed at Kadesh. There Miriam died and was buried."

They were back at Kadesh Barnea. Time for take two. But before heading out, Miriam, Moses' oldest sister, died and was buried. We remember the precocious, courageous girl who asked Pharaoh's daughter if she wanted her to get a nurse. Quick on her feet, she made it possible for Jochebed to care for baby Moses for a few years. The Bible mentions Miriam's death because it was a significant loss, a passing of the old guard.

Along with Miriam, they lost their water supply. This unexpected shortage disturbed and angered the people. Numbers 20:3-5 says, "They quarreled with Moses and said, 'If only we had died when our brothers fell dead before the Lord! Why did you bring the Lord's community into this wilderness, that we and our livestock should die here? Why did you bring us up out of Egypt to this terrible place?... There is no water to drink!'"

We have names for our generations: the Baby Boomers, Generation X, the Millennials, Gen Z, and Generation Alpha. For Israel, the previous generation was "The Doubters." Here was "Generation Next," but not much had changed. They continued to quarrel, beating their leader with the same old stick, "Can't you do better than this? Why did we ever follow you? How could you be so lame?" Sadly, they followed the example of their parents. Not knowing what to do, Moses and Aaron went to the tent of meeting and fell down before the Lord.

In Numbers 20:8, God gave the following instructions, "Take the staff, and you and your brother Aaron gather the assembly together. Speak to that rock before their eyes and it will pour out its water..." Moses had been here before. Just after leaving Egypt, the people threw a fit over the lack of water. As God directed, he struck the rock once, and water flowed. But here, at the end of a long career, God threw a changeup. "Don't strike. Just speak the word and water will flow." The command was clear. God's promise was sure.

But notice Numbers 20:10-11, "He and Aaron gathered the assembly together in front of the rock and Moses said to them, 'Listen, you rebels, must we bring you water out of this rock?' Then Moses raised his arm and struck the rock twice with his staff. Water gushed out, and the community and their livestock drank."

Mission accomplished. Touchdown. Water for the community. But God was not pleased. In Exodus 20:12, the Lord said to Moses, "Because you did not trust in me enough to honor me as holy in the sight of the Israelites, you will not bring this community into the land I give them.'"

The banishment God dished out seems too severe for one so faithful. I remember one little blunder that disqualified me from going to see a movie. The year was 1978, and the first Superman movie starring Christopher Reeves had just come out. I was a youngster playing in the church parking lot after service when the adults decided to see the man of steel on the big screen. We were elated, jumping, and slapping high fives.

My friends and I sat in the back of the station wagon on the way to the theater. Somehow the word "butt" came up, which all made us laugh. We began to vamp on anything that had to do with butts: butt cheeks, butt cheese, butt head, etc. That's when an adult on the team called us out. We laughed and told them it was in the Bible. But dad was not happy, and turned the car around. Back at the church parking lot, he sent the rest to the theater while we went home. I blew up in tears and pleaded for grace. While dad snuggled in his chair with a book and a cup of coffee, I sat in the kitchen and cried my eyes out. All because I said the word "butt."

We don't know what God saw. We don't know what was in Moses' heart. We do know that God holds his leaders to a higher standard. James 3:1 says, "Not many of you should become teachers, my brothers, for you know that we who teach will be judged with greater strictness." It's sobering to think we can lose it all in the blink of an eye. Let's remember he gave us everything we have, and he can take it all away. As Proverbs 9:10 says, "The fear of the Lord is the beginning of wisdom."

Truth #14—Make every effort to protect God's call on your life.

How precious is God's call—the plan, the mission, his dream pulsating in our heart. Second Peter 1:10 instructs us, "Therefore, my brothers and sisters, make every effort to confirm your calling and election. For if you do these things, you will never stumble." Notice the promise, "You will never stumble." You will never be the guy who fumbles the baton, trips on his shoelace, and falls flat on his face just before the finish line. But the promise has a condition, "If you do these things." What things? Make every effort to confirm your calling. No exceptions, short cuts, or special dispensations for yourself because you've been in it for so long, and have sacrificed so much. With each year, with every lap, by God's grace, confirm, establish, and protect the call. So, what does that look like?

First, remember the evidence of trust is obedience. Somehow, Moses' capacity to trust had withered. God told Moses to speak to the rock, but he decided to use his staff instead. He doubted God's word and disobeyed his command.

Maybe Moses' thought process went something like, "It's been forty years. Look at me. Still the same old battles. They still think I'm a lame leader. Maybe I should try it my way for once."

Maybe he played the movie in his mind. "Imagine calling the grumbling camp together, filled with my critics and naysayers. What if I say, 'Water come forth!' and nothing happens? A blunder for the ages!" Instead of doing exactly what God said, he struck the rock with his staff like he did years before, adding one more for good measure. God wanted to do a new miracle in a new way, but Moses wasn't willing to change. Again, God said in Numbers 20:12, "Because you did not trust in me enough to honor me as holy in the sight of the Israelites…"

In 2012, scientists from NASA released a photograph of the farthest ever look into deep space, called the Hubble Ultra Deep Field. Like countless sparkling jewels on a black backdrop, the picture revealed thousands of galaxies never before seen in stunning colors of red, blue, green, white, and yellow. Up until this photograph, it was believed the universe contained eight, ten, maybe twelve thousand galaxies. With the universe expanding in all directions, they believe the total number is around two trillion!

Here's an even more incredible realization—the God who made those two trillion galaxies cares for you. What a mighty God we serve! The one who holds the universe together knows the number of hairs on your head. If he cares enough to feed the birds and clothe the dirt with grass, how much more will he care for us. There's no one more trustworthy.

How do we know we really trust God? We simply do what he says, whether we feel like it or not. So each day, let's make Psalm 25:1 our prayer, "In you, Lord my God, I put my trust."

Second, protect your heart from anger and bitterness. Not only did Moses not trust God enough, it looks like he still wrestled with his anger issues. We can hear it in his words, "Listen, you rebels!"

(Numbers 20:10) At the end of his journey, Moses had an episode of wilderness rage.

Have you ever been so furious you wanted to smash something? Numbers 20:11 says, "Moses raised his arms and struck the rock twice with his staff." The Hebrew word for "strike" is *nakah*, and it can also mean "to hit, beat, slay, kill, or smash." After God commanded him to speak, Moses smashed the rock instead. In response God said, "You will not bring the people into the land I give them."

Moses had smashed things before. When he was 40, he smote the Egyptian and buried his body. Later, when he saw the golden calf at Mount Sinai, he shattered the tablets engraved with the finger of God. With the finish line in sight, his old shortcoming reared its ugly head.

I'm thinking he was probably angry with God. Pastor Moses had been doing portable church in the desert for the last 40 years. Their place of worship was a tent with lots of poles and curtains. Lots of set up and take down. To find his church you had to follow the cloud. But who would want to join such a negative team? All their church potlucks were the same—leftover manna and quail. The frustration with the slow pace of God's blessing finally boiled over and Moses struck the rock.

Here's the scary thing about leading angry. It works. The wife does what you want. The husband retreats to his cave. The kids clean the kitchen. The yard gets mowed. The water comes gushing out. And we can start to like it that way. The rush of power feels good. But bitter, angry leaders who smash and ram things through will never reach the Promised Land God has for them.

Third, to confirm our calling, live to make Jesus famous. Could it be that Moses was tired of the belittling criticisms of the people? Speaking to the rock was so passive. So he opted for a public display of personal power and slammed the rock—like a basketball player who dunks and hangs on the rim to shatter the backboard. "Who's your daddy now?" Notice how Moses took the credit in Numbers 20:10, "Listen, you rebels, must we bring you water out of this rock?"

Re-read God's response in Numbers 20:12, "Because you did not trust in me enough to honor me as holy in the sight of the Israelites, you will not bring this community into the land I give them." In the sight of the people, Moses took the honor that belonged to God.

For those who have the responsibility to minister in front of others, let's not make the platform a place to perform. When we're done preaching or singing, we don't want people leaving church talking about our shoes, the size of our biceps, our skinny jeans, or how tight our flop over looked. We want them caught up in the glory of our Savior. The mission of our ministry is to make Jesus famous.

A divine miracle was about to happen. Water would flow from a rock. That's when Moses inserted himself and said, "Look what we're going to do." If the miracle finally happens, if the financial breakthrough comes, if people start pouring in, if your social platform finally grows, don't make yourselves the Savior. Proverbs 16:18 says, "Pride goes before destruction, a haughty spirit before a fall." First Peter 5:6 says, "God resists the proud but gives grace to the humble." Continue to give honor where honor is due.

Johann Sebastian Bach was one of the greatest composers in history (1685-1750). His music is studied in every conservatory and is still performed and recorded by the world's most talented musicians. The chord progressions in his works have influenced every genre, including pop, jazz, and modern worship music.

In his life, J. S. Bach was a church organist and choir director. Each week he composed original music for the congregation. As he used his musical gift, he felt his soul worshipping God. He once said, "I play the notes as they are written, but it is God who makes the music."

Bach was never famous in his lifetime. Eighty years after his death, in 1829, the composer Felix Mendelssohn found a copy of Bach's "St. Matthew Passion" (the story of Jesus' death and resurrection) and performed it. Finally, the word spread and churches all over the world began performing his music.

At the end of every piece he composed, Bach always wrote, "Solo Deo Gloria," which means, "Only to God's glory." Bach didn't concern himself with fame. In using his gifts, he wanted to bring glory to God alone. May the same be true for us.

Deuteronomy 34:10 summarizes the impact of Moses' ministry – "Since then, no prophet has risen in Israel like Moses, whom the LORD knew face to face." In the Old Testament, Moses stands out above the rest. Yet even after all the books, answered prayers, and miracles, his righteous record was marred with flaws.

But in love, God sent another prophet in Jesus. Hebrews 3:3 says, "Jesus has been found worthy of greater honor than Moses, just as the builder of a house has greater honor than the house itself." Jesus deserves greater honor because he gave what Moses could never give. By faith, his perfect righteousness is freely given to all who believe.

If Moses couldn't live the perfect life, let's not fool ourselves. Instead of striving, receive this priceless gift. Philippians 3:9 says, "And be found in him, not having a righteousness of my own that comes from the law, but that which is through faith in Christ—the righteousness that comes from God on the basis of faith."

I don't know where you've stumbled today. I don't know if you blew it during the final lap. But I do know there is grace for every failure. It's time to get back up and run again.

15

The Final Climb

> "Instead, they were longing for a better country—a heavenly one. Therefore God is not ashamed to be called their God, for he has prepared a city for them." (Hebrews 11:16)

The book of Deuteronomy ends with this lofty statement about Moses' legacy, "For no one has ever shown the mighty power or performed the awesome deeds that Moses did in the sight of all Israel." (Deuteronomy 34:12) Moses performed wondrous deeds by God's mighty power. But his journey came to an end. Deuteronomy 34:7 says, "Moses was a hundred and twenty years old when he died, yet his eyes were not weak nor his strength gone." At 120 years old, he still had the twinkle of curiosity. I'm sure he had a project or two he wanted to complete. But it was time to go home.

The oldest person on record to ever live in modern times was Jeanne Louise Calment from Arles, France. Born on February 21, 1875, she lived 122 years and 164 days. When she was 120, someone asked her what she expected in the future. She said, "I expect a short one." She survived two world wars and the Spanish Flu. In her 80's she took up fencing and continued to cycle in her 100's, but finally died on August 4, 1997.

If you take your multivitamins and eat organic fruits and vegetables, maybe you reach 100. But like there's only a limited number of Swedish Fish in a bag, at some point we'll reach our final day. That's why the psalmist taught us to pray in Psalm 90:17, "Teach us to number our days, that we may gain a heart of wisdom."

Lesson #15–To finish well, start each day with the end in mind.

Deuteronomy 34:1 says, "Then Moses climbed Mount Nebo from the plains of Moab to the top of Pisgah, across from Jericho. There the Lord showed him the whole land." What the Lord promised over forty years before, he finally saw with his eyes. Mount Nebo is located just east of the Jordan River and is the highest in a cluster of Pisgah summits. From the top, Moses could see past the Jordan to the Mediterranean Sea. Stretching out before him was the Promised Land, the culminating vision of his ministry.

When he was an 80-year-old shepherd, he stood by the burning bush and heard God say in Exodus 3:8, "So I have come down to rescue them from the hand of the Egyptians and to bring them up out of that land into a good and spacious land, a land flowing with milk and honey." There were major setbacks over the last 40 years. Most disappointing of all was the rebellion of the previous generation, when they chose to believe the bad report. But still, Moses pressed on. Propelled forward by God's vision, he finally saw the realization of his dream.

What is a vision? A vision is a mental picture of a preferable future made possible by God's power. It's something we see first with eyes of faith. It is the end result of our life's work. Before we can touch the brick and mortar, feel the softness of the carpet and warmth of the lights, we picture it in our mind. Instead of seeing things as they are, we see things as they can be.

A great example of this is Bill Irwin. At 50 years of age, he became the first blind hiker to cross the Appalachian Trail, a stretch of more than 2,100 miles from Georgia to Maine. His only guide was his German shepherd named Orient. Midway through his life, Bill Irwin lost his eyesight. He smoked five packs a day and was an alcoholic. While sitting in drug rehab with his son, Bill finally acknowledged the depth of his addiction. He committed his life to Jesus and found new hope.

Though he was blind, Bill discovered how much he liked the outdoors. Later, he heard a sermon on 2 Corinthians 5:7, "For we walk by faith, not by sight." A vision was born to hike the full length of the great trail. He fell a thousand times over the eight-month journey, but finally made it to the top on November 21, 1990. Though Bill Irwin was blind, he had vision. Before it became a reality, he saw it with spiritual eyes.

As you journey through life are you facing any obstacles? Like Moses, you may be surrounded by a multitude of naysayers. They may even be members of your own family. The only consistent thing you're seeing is inconsistency in the world around you. Everything is uncertain. Here's some advice. Ask God for vision. Pray this prayer, "Lord help me see how it can be by your power." In other words, begin with the end in mind.

Here are some questions to help you get the ball rolling. What does my Promised Land look like? On the day I leave this world for the next, what mountain will I have climbed? How do I want to be remembered? What will the quality of my friendships be? What will my relationship with God be like? What do I want my spouse and kids to say about me after I'm gone? What kind of contribution do I want to make for the glory of God?

Picture the end. Give yourself permission to dream. Ephesians 3:20 says, "Now to him who is able to do immeasurably more than all we ask or imagine, according to his power that is at work within us."

As you set out on your next step it's important to see yourself as a servant of God. Deuteronomy 34:5 says, "And Moses the servant of the Lord died there in Moab, as the Lord had said." The title most often used for Moses is not lawgiver, deliverer, miracle worker, or author, but servant of God. Servants do not choose their assignments. They don't come with demands and conditions.

When God told Moses he would not lead the Israelites into Canaan, it was a major disappointment. In a most revealing passage, in Deuteronomy 3:23 Moses said, "At that time I pleaded with the Lord...Let me go over and see the good land beyond the Jordan – that fine hill country and Lebanon." Moses prayed many powerful prayers in his life. His intercession moved the heart of God. Here he pleaded for God to reconsider, but God said in Deuteronomy 3:26, "That is enough...Do not speak to me anymore about this matter."

As God's servant, Moses humbly set aside his plans. Life consists of many unexpected changes—demotions, promotions, closed and open doors. If God takes something away, that means he has something better in store. Don't insist on your little plans when he has a much greater assignment waiting. While Moses wanted Canaan, God wanted him home to be in his presence, the place of everlasting rest and joy.

We like titles: reverend, bishop, doctor, apostle. But people do not follow titles. They follow servants. Jesus was the most influential leader in history. But the Bible never says, "he took on the nature of a leader." Philippians 2:7 says, "Rather, he made himself nothing by taking the very nature of a servant." As you see the end, and set your goals, hold them loosely in your hands. God may have something far better for your future.

As you take those steps with the end in mind, remember this is a long haul. When the hard times hit, keep hanging on. Moses had the privilege of spending weeks on the mountain top in communion with God. But for most of his ministry, he lived with the people as they journeyed through the desert. At one point, he asked God to take his life as he cried out, "Why have you brought this trouble on your servant? What have I done to displease you that you put the burden of these people on me?" (Numbers 11:11; 13) But God gave Moses the grace to persevere.

In Ron Chernow's biography, *Washington*, he writes about the darkest moment in the American Revolution—the winter of 1777. The British had chased the Continental army from Philadelphia and retired there for the winter to enjoy its comforts. In that time, it was common to break from warfare during the cold, allowing officers to enjoy concerts, plays, and parties. Washington's army was small, under-resourced, and on the verge of dissolution. While the Redcoats enjoyed Philadelphia's food, entertainment, and warmth, Washington made the tough decision to stay with his men through the long winter months at a place forever remembered as Valley Forge.

The men set out right away to build winter quarters. Over 2000 log cabins were set up in a few short weeks, huts about 14 by 16 feet. The ceilings were six and a half feet high and could house about 12 soldiers. Washington was concerned about their survival. Walking into Valley Forge, he saw streaks of blood in the snow from soldiers with no shoes.

As winter fell, the struggling army took the appearance of a collection of homeless beggars. Food was scarce, as neighboring farmers sold their crops and supplies to the enemy instead of giving them away to the penniless Continental army. The men often ate what were called "fire cakes," blobs of flour and water baked on hot stones. Soldiers had rags for clothes and no blankets to protect them from winter winds. Horses died, and their rotting bodies lay on the snow, filling the air with the smell of decay. The soldiers felt forsaken and discouraged.

Washington could have taken a leave of absence to his warm Mount Vernon estate. But his presence inspired his soldiers and fanned the flames of liberty throughout the colonies. At their lowest point, a Prussian captain named Baron von Steuben appeared. He knew how to train, drill, organize, and instill discipline. He gave the troops a sense of purpose while they waited.

They drilled all day long at the center of camp, as von Steuben spewed a torrent of profanities. By winter's end, the army knew how to turn in formation, and switch from line to column and back to line. Through that time of shared suffering, the Continental army would rise stronger and more determined. The most significant victory of the Revolution was not on a battlefield, but at Valley Forge.

When you persevere, you don't go around, over, or under difficulty. You go through tough times to the other side. As we hold on to God in hardship our grip grows stronger. The prolonged pressure enlarges our capacity for more. In the end we have a fresh determination and greater courage.

Notice the description of Moses at the end in Deuteronomy 34:7, "Moses was a hundred and twenty years old when he died, yet his eyes were not weak nor his strength gone." It's almost like God had to unplug him and say, "OK. We're done. On to your next assignment." While his skin sagged with age, his spirit was alert and alive. The fire of his first love still burned bright. James 1:12 says, "Blessed is the one who perseveres under trial because, having stood the test, that person will receive the crown of life that the Lord has promised to those who love him."

If we're going to begin each day with the end in mind, we must also let go of the past. Though Moses never used the word "forgive," we see it lived out. Over and over, he prayed for God to bless the ones who wounded him the most. His life is a good illustration of 1 Peter 4:8, "Above all, love one another deeply, because love covers over a multitude of sins."

My son and I recently went deep-sea fishing with a friend. We took his boat about ten miles offshore. Down below was a large reef, what anglers call "structure." We hooked chunks of squid and sank them to the bottom. After sitting for about an hour, my son's pole began to bob. It was like Christmas morning as he began reeling in his gift. To our surprise, the rod bent over, and the drag started to scream. Before he could set himself, our friend ran across the deck and took the pole out of his hands. As Arlie stood there, he reeled in his fish—a two-and-a-half foot barracuda.

On the way home, there wasn't much talking. My son finally spoke up, "He took the rod out of my hands! He reeled in my fish." A few weeks later, it came up again, "Remember, when I caught that barracuda and my pole was taken away? That was my fish. That was my one chance to reel in a big one, and he took it away." Months later, it came up again, "Remember how he reeled in my fish?" So we stopped right there and had a little talk about forgiveness.

One sign of unforgiveness is remembering. You bring it up and keep it fresh. In the New Testament, the Greek word *aphiemi* is often translated as "forgive." But it can also mean "to send away, to let go, or release." Offense shows up on the doorsteps of our heart like a homeless kitten wanting to come in and snuggle. The kitten will grow into an angry lion. If you feel like someone took your pole, take a stand. Look at the offense and say, "You're not coming in. Go away!"

For those who know Jesus as Lord and Savior, our ultimate end is more glorious than we could ever dream. Our true Promised Land is not an earthly accomplishment, possession, promotion, or piece of real estate. It's our heavenly home, a place of unimaginable beauty and unfathomable joy. Our journey through the wilderness of this life is nothing compared to our eternal home on the other side.

Like Moses fixed his eyes on Canaan, we must live with heaven in mind. Colossians 3:1-2 says, "Set your minds on things above, not on earthly things." In Hebrews 11, the heroes of faith who finished well did so because, "they looked forward to a city with foundations, whose architect and builder is God." (Hebrews 11:10)

Many believe thinking on heaven will make us worthless in life. But when heaven is on our mind, we know our time is short. We want to make the most of every opportunity. We have boldness to take risks and step out in faith. We strive for holiness because we know soon we'll stand in the presence God. Remember, heaven is promised to you. It is your inheritance. Live today in the light of your glorious future as a child of God.

I remember when Wendy and I got engaged back in 1998. Her wedding day was a moment she had dreamed about since childhood. She went to work quickly making detailed plans for the ceremony and reception, while my job was planning the honeymoon.

I knew we both loved the beach, so I chose Maui. We had one major obstacle. Because our wedding was in August, the tickets were sky high. Going to Maui looked impossible, so I started thinking about Virginia Beach. A month before our wedding day, my parents pulled a huge surprise. They gave us two tickets to Maui, with a return date of two weeks! As it turned out, they had a ton of frequent flyer miles, and generously gave those to us. But these were not just tickets. They were first-class tickets! When we finally landed in paradise, I didn't want to get off the plane.

As I reflect back on that gift, it fills my heart with thankfulness. What could be better than two weeks in Maui as newlyweds? Actually, there is something that blows Maui, Bora Bora, or Rio de Janeiro away—the paradise of our eternal home.

We could never afford those tickets. But God graciously made a way. Through faith in Jesus Christ we have reserved, first-class seats to heaven. Our tickets were purchased by the blood of Jesus when he died on the cross, paying the price for our sins. He did that out of love so that we could be with him forever. Romans 6:23 says, "For the wages of sin is death, but the gift of God is eternal life in Christ Jesus our Lord."

For some reason the words "life calendar" popped into my head the other day. So I Googled it and up came an article from the Huffington

Post called, "Your Life in Weeks." Here's a visual representation of a 90-year life.

A 90-Year Human Life in Years

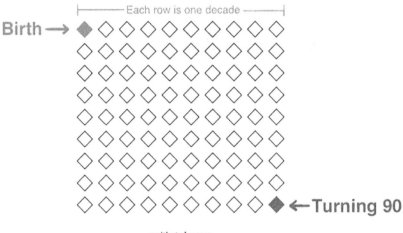

Then, the article showed a 90-year life in months. Notice each row represents three years. These pictures are not meant to discourage you, but to bring you face to face with reality. Our life journey is short and precious.

A 90-Year Human Life in Months

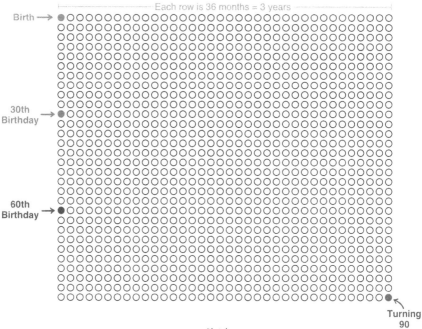

Pray today for vision. Forgive your offenders so you can focus on your future. May you see yourself as a servant of God. When difficulty hits, hold on. We can't imagine what God has in store for us. "No eye has seen, no ear has heard, and no mind has imagined what God has prepared for those who love him." (1 Corinthians 2:9) God is taking you somewhere. By his grace you can win in the wilderness and reach the Promised Land.

CPSIA information can be obtained
at www.ICGtesting.com
Printed in the USA
BVHW092320060922
646311BV00016B/805